CROCKPOT FREEZER COOKBOOK

Best Freezable Meals Recipes for Busy Family

(Delicious and Easy Recipes to Feed Your Whole Family)

Mark Root

Published by Alex Howard

© **Mark Root**

All Rights Reserved

Crockpot Freezer Cookbook: Best Freezable Meals Recipes for Busy Family (Delicious and Easy Recipes to Feed Your Whole Family)

ISBN 978-1-990169-55-7

All rights reserved. No part of this guide may be reproduced in any form without permission in writing from the publisher except in the case of brief quotations embodied in critical articles or reviews.

Legal & Disclaimer

The information contained in this book is not designed to replace or take the place of any form of medicine or professional medical advice. The information in this book has been provided for educational and entertainment purposes only.

The information contained in this book has been compiled from sources deemed reliable, and it is accurate to the best of the Author's knowledge; however, the Author cannot guarantee its accuracy and validity and cannot be held liable for any errors or omissions. Changes are periodically made to this book. You must consult your doctor or get professional medical advice before using any of the suggested remedies, techniques, or information in this book.

Table of contents

Part 1 1

Introduction 2

Breakfast 47

Baked Oatmeal 48

Breakfast Burritos 49

Chocolate Chip Scones 51

Apple Buttermilk Muffins 53

Breakfast Sandwiches 55

Sausage Breakfast Sandwiches 57

Simple Pancakes 59

Streusel Topped Banana Bread 61

Very Berry Fruit Smoothie 63

Cinnamon Chip Scones 65

Appetizers 67

Hot Pizza Dip 67

Bbq Chicken Wings 69

Baked Mozzarella Bites 70

Jalapeno Poppers 72

Hummus 74

Sausage Wonton Cups 75

- Part 2 76
- Homemade Chicken Bowls 77
- Spinach & Noodle Casserole 79
- Sirloin & Okra Stew 81
- Pepperoni Pizza Puffs 83
- Easy Casserole 85
- Shrimp Spaghetti 86
- Beef Kebabs 88
- Sweet Pea & Chicken Pasta 90
- Jacks Sausage & Shrimp 92
- Chicken Drumsticks 94
- Dumplings With Chicken 97
- Seafood Tortillas 99
- European Meatball Stew 101
- Beef Pot 103
- Grans Sausage Pie 105
- Chicken Tandoori & Couscous 107
- Beef Meatloaf 109
- Chicken Casserole 111
- Mexican Turkey Casserole 113
- Beef Moussaka 115

Greek Lamb Meatballs 117

Great Lamb Dish 119

Hot Pilafs 121

Mixed Bolognese 122

Turkey Sausage Gumbo 124

Chicken Lasagna 126

Turkey Pasta 128

Pork & Mushrooms 131

Original Chicken Tikka Masala 133

Mama's Stuffed Peppers 135

Easy Chicken Pizzas 137

Mexican Chili 139

Asian Curry Stew 141

Spiced Chicken Casserole 142

Sausage Calzones 145

White Beans With Pork 147

Vegetarian Empanadas 149

French Onion Soup For Slow Cooker 151

Easy Minestrone Soup 152

Sausage - Sage Soup 154

Charming Chicken 156

Peanut Chicken Curry 156

Prunes With Chicken 157

Teriyaki Chicken 158

Sweet Bbq Chicken 159

Dijon Chicken 160

Garlic Lime Chicken 160

Pineapple Chicken 161

Chicken &Black Beans 162

Bbq Orange Chicken 163

Sticky Apricot Chicken 163

Pleasant Pork 164

Pepper Pork 164

Bbq Baby Back Ribs 165

Ham Soup 166

Sweet & Sour Pork 168

Honey Maple Pork Ribs 169

Sweet Soy & Ketchup Pork Chops 169

Pineapple Pork Roast 170

Balsamic Pork 171

Ham & Corn Chowder 172

Vegetable Pork Stew 173

Beloved Beef 174

Sloppy Joes 174

Spicy Shredded Beef 175

Amazing Beef Stew 176

Mediterranean Brisket 177

Beef Stroganoff 178

Mozzarella Meatloaf With Mushrooms & Pepperoni 179

Pepper Steak Roast 180

Beef Cocktail Cranberry Meatballs 182

Beef Chili 183

Beef & Veggie Curry 184

Superb Seafood 185

Seafood Chowder 185

Scrumptious Shrimp & Chicken 186

Citrus Fish 188

Shrimp & Chicken Jambalaya 189

Sweet & Sour Shrimp 190

Part 1

Introduction

We are all busy these days as we run from work to home, to practices and family obligations. It can be very hard, if not downright impossible to put dinner on the table each night. Fast food restaurants have helped us solve this dilemma by providing us with inexpensive and quick meals that get us back on the road quickly.

The problem is that as more and more of us have indulged in this quick-fix method of solving the dinnertime dilemma, our waistlines have expanded, our rate of disease has increased and we have created a nation of overweight and inactive children.

If you could provide your family with home-cooked "fast food" meals, wouldn't you choose that option instead? If you spend just a few hours in the kitchen each month (or a couple of hours each week), you can create a number of homemade meals that can be on the table in less than 30 minutes each night. You save prep time, mess and energy. And we won't even mention the money you'll save. (But you WILL save money!)

What is freezer cooking, anyway?

What do we mean when we say "freezer cooking"?

Freezer cooking can mean a lot of things -- cooking with ingredients that are already frozen (such as store-bought bread dough and vegetables), reheating pre-cooked meals for a quick meal anytime, or putting frozen components together to create a fresh meal on the fly.

The good news is that none of these methods is wrong and all qualify for the title of "freezer cooking," That's because freezer cooking is highly flexible and versatile. You can make freezer cooking to be anything you want it to be, customize it to your needs and create a workable plan for quick meals anytime.

Beginners to freezer cooking often follow a pre-made plan. For example, they might follow a "hamburger plan" or a "chicken plan." The plan might include a number of dishes that use that protein; in the end, you'll have dishes that all feature this protein prominently.

The unfortunate reality, however, is often you won't like all of the dishes in the plan. In fact, you might only end up liking a few. So while you benefited by having all those quick meals on hand, you might decide that the downside – the dislike of half the dishes or more – isn't worth the convenience.

In frustration, you might return to Plan A, which is all about the status quo. Even if the status quo isn't working well, you return to it because at least you know you can prepare family favorites when you do cook and you can eat out when you don't have time to cook.

The good news? If you learn the basics of freezer cooking, you will soon learn how to adapt those family favorites into freezer recipes. Now you will get the advantage of quick meals that are in the freezer and ready to go and made to your likes and dietary needs.

You'll soon learn that nearly every recipe can be frozen, if you know how to adapt it.

Misconceptions

Head to any bookstore and pick up a freezer cookbook. You will likely find it filled with recipes that are more casserole in nature than fresh meals. Many people don't particularly like casseroles and so this method of cooking isn't conducive to their style of eating.

While there's nothing inherently wrong with chicken and rice casseroles or enchilada dishes, a lot of people don't want to eat casseroles often. While these casseroles might fulfill the need for comfort food, they are hardly "everyday" meals that people want to eat frequently. If you don't look hard, you might think that there are few alternatives for freezer cooking and give up on the concept immediately.

The good news is that freezer cooking has changed in recent years to allow for more flexibility and fresh cooking in the kitchen. You can freeze components of a recipe and cook when it's time to eat. While you don't avoid cooking altogether, you can save a great deal of time because at mealtime you won't have to measure anything, cut meat, or do other prep work.

Here's what you can expect to learn in this book:

- The pros and cons of freezer cooking
- What can you freeze?
- Tips for freezer storage
- Tips for freezer cooking
- A sample freezer cooking session
- Tips and tricks for successful freezer cooking for the long haul
- More than 80 recipes that can be frozen for quick meals and snacks anytime

Let's get started because once we sell you on freezer cooking, we'll bet you will want to get started right away!

Pros and Cons of Freezer Cooking

It's possible that we are biased, but we think that freezer cooking really speaks for itself. Once you understand what it's about and how it works, we think you'll be hard pressed to argue against the benefits of freezer cooking.

But let's look at some pros and cons of freezer cooking anyhow. (Just know going in that we can debunk all of the cons.)

Six Reasons to Cook for the Freezer (the pros).

1. You'll save money.

Saving money is perhaps one of the biggest incentives for cooking for the freezer. When you cook for the freezer, you can buy items in bulk and have little waste. Because you do all of your shopping in bulk, you can take advantage of bulk discounts and save a great deal of money.

Let's look specifically at how you might save money by freezer shopping. Say you see a great deal on boneless, skinless chicken breasts. You have a number of recipes you like to make with chicken, from chicken divan to chicken fajitas to grilled chicken. You realize that you can take advantage of the sale (which requires you to buy in bulk in order to get the discount) and do a freezer session.

While shopping for the chicken, you pick up a number of other items you need to complete your session. This might include onions (which you can purchase in a bag instead of loose, which saves money), as well as tomatoes, which you can buy in a large can at a warehouse store for significantly less than you might spend at the grocery store.

You buy 10 pounds of the chicken breast, spend $25, and spend another $40 on ingredients. At the end of your cooking session, you have 10 bags of various freezer meals and components for your family of 4. This means you have spent $6.50 on each meal, or roughly $1.62 to feed each person. You'd be hard pressed to meet this price when cooking dinner fresh each night and you certainly can't do it when you pick up pizza or fast food each night.

If you have an income that fluctuates or is unpredictable, you can do a freezer session when you have a good income and stock up for the low-income periods. This saves money, but also saves you from having to indulge in beans and rice for dinners during the dry spell.

2. You'll save time.

Once you start freezer cooking, you might find yourself amazed with how much time you can save. Perhaps you favor simple meals at home. You like to come home, throw some chicken in a bag with marinade and let it sit for 30 minutes while you cook rice and make a salad. After 30 minutes, you put the chicken on the grill and 20 minutes later, you can enjoy your fresh meal.

Let's examine the real time cost of prepping dinner this way. To make this dinner, you:

- Open the package of chicken and trim the chicken
- Measure out perhaps 5 ingredients for a simple marinade and mince garlic
- Measure out and place rice in a pot to cook
- Chop lettuce and other vegetables and mix them for salad

All of this might take 20 minutes of hands-on time. This is time you could spend walking the dog, watching the news or reading with a child. If you have freezer meals prepped, you can instead:

- Pull the thawed and marinated chicken out of the refrigerator and put it on the grill
- Heat up pre-cooked rice that you pulled from the freezer the night before
- Prep the salad

All of this might take 5 minutes of hands-on time, is just as fresh as the first meal and reduces the number of dishes you get dirty, thus saving you clean-up time, as well as prep time.

Imagine how much time you'll save on meals that aren't quite this simple. Add that up over a week or a month and rejoice. You'll get so much time back!

3. It's healthy.

Contrary to what you might think, freezer cooking isn't only about cooking with "cream of" this and "cream of" that soup and other mixes. You won't find one can of "cream of" anything required for any recipe in this book. You will find one or two recipes that contain a packet of seasoning mix, but that's about as far as it goes for pre-packaged ingredients.

You might not mind the "cream of" anything soups, but we like freezer recipes that are a little fresher, and a little more healthy.

Aside from the recipes in this book, you can make freezer cooking as healthy as you like. If you mostly prefer just chicken and brown rice for dinner, you can create freezer recipes that suit this need. If you have allergies, you can customize recipes to your needs.

Even those who diet can find freezer cooking beneficial. In fact, you might find it hard to stay on some diets without utilizing at least some freezer cooking techniques. All of that food prep can take time, but you can cut down on some time by prepping some of the food for the freezer and simply working on a daily basis with the rest.

Freezer cooking can be as healthy as you want to make it. If you have special dietary restrictions (or preferences) you can adjust recipes to suit your needs or adjust the recipes in this book to meet your needs. Freezer cooking is flexible enough to work with you as you like.

4. You can cook specific to your family's needs.

Picky eater in the family? We know how stressful that can be. Many families with a picky eater will choose to eat in restaurants more than they eat at home. This way even the picky eater can find something that suits his or her tastes.

But eating in restaurants all the time is expensive, time consuming and unhealthy. It sets a bad precedent as well. Your kids and other family members will assume that the only way to get a good meal is to eat out. Instead, you can make freezer cooking work for you even here.

If you learn to freezer cook, you can fill a freezer with family favorites, as well as favorites for the picky eater. If you normally spend extra time making food for the picky eater while making a completely different meal for the family, you can save time by having the picky eater's favorite things handy in the freezer, thereby reducing your stress and saving money.

Maybe you like to have pizza every Friday night, but the idea of making pizza from scratch gets you down after a long week. You might end up at the local pizza parlor. But that adds up and you hate spending that much money every Friday. Did you know you can fill your freezer with pizza dough, pizza toppings (including the sauce) and cheese? Then all you have to do is pull out whatever you need for that Friday and make pizza at home. Kids love making their own pizzas. Maybe you'll create a new family tradition!

5. It makes entertaining easy.

Do you like to entertain? Do you usually cook everything from scratch? If you do, we bow to you, because we know how hard that is. If you don't cook from scratch each time you entertain, where do you get the food? Do you buy prepared food from the warehouse store or grocery store? Do you buy frozen food? Do you hire a caterer?

You might be surprised to learn that you can make and freeze dozens of appetizers, sweet treats and other entertaining-friendly dishes so all you have to do it thaw, heat and eat. Talk about effortless entertaining!

Aside from planned entertaining, freezer cooking can help with unplanned entertaining – you know, when someone unexpected comes over for dinner? What do you normally do? If you call the pizza guy or resort to spaghetti because you just don't know what else to do, you're not alone. That's a common solution for many people.

When you freezer cook, though, you can race home, search through the freezer, see which things can be thawed in the microwave and rush a home-cooked and yummy dinner to the table. Your guests will never know it came from the freezer. Everyone wins!

6. Reduces stress.

If you love to cook, we give you a high five. You might really love getting dinner on the table each night. But even those who love to cook can't do it every night and often you don't want do. Or maybe you can't stand cooking, think you are a bad cook and you stress every single night about what to put on the table.

No matter your situation, you'll find that freezer cooking works for you. Knowing that you have dozens of choices in the freezer can easily reduce stress in a significant way. If you love to cook, you can take a day off every now and then while still providing your family with a home-cooked meal. As well, you can put some of your favorite dishes in the freezer and save time later. If you are very busy, it can be hard to find time to get in the kitchen no matter how much you love it. Freezer cooking solves this dilemma.

If you hate to cook, you can force yourself in the kitchen every now and then to create a number of freezer-friendly dishes and then stay distant from the kitchen for weeks on end. If you really don't like to cook, you'll probably want to choose recipes like Garlic Beef Enchiladas or Southern Style Smothered Pork Chops – recipes that require heating only on the day you eat them.

Someone who really enjoys cooking, on the other hand, might like to keep components of recipes on hand, like those for Chicken Fajitas. That way, you can still get into the kitchen and give a hands-on approach to putting dinner on the table.

No matter what your situation and preferences, it's likely that you experience at least a little stress at least some of the time over dinner. Freezer cooking can help you in whatever way you choose.

7. You can help others.

When you have pre-made, homemade food in the freezer, you can help others when they need it. You can bring meals to new mothers, or to friends who have suffered a loss. You can help someone who might be in a difficult situation.

This might not be a good motivation to get into freezer cooking, but it can end up being a wonderful side benefit.

Reasons Why You Might Not Want to Freezer Cook

We admit there might be arguments against freezer cooking, so let's examine those now. Here are three reasons you might not want to freezer cook.

8. You can't find time to do it.

This is a legitimate concern. Let's look at this in detail.

First, a lot of freezer cooks will designate a specific day to do their freezer cooking each month. They might decide that they'll do their freezer session for the month on the first Saturday of the month. This can be a great way to handle time, because you not only know that you should have your session planned by that first Saturday, but it allows you to plan your session based on the four weeks in between sessions. You will be able to easily identify which day you should do your shopping and how that relates to the cooking day. But this might not work for you.

Another way to handle freezer cooking is to cook when you have time. You might realize on a Tuesday that you are not only getting low on freezer dishes, but that you have Sunday available for cooking. You can spend some time during the week coming up with the recipes you want to make, creating a grocery list, grocery shopping and even doing some pre-prep.

Perhaps you don't like the idea of giving up an entire day to create a few weeks or months' worth of recipes. What then? You can do what many freezer cooks do – improvise.

Improvising in this situation means that you might instead create double recipes of your favorite recipes as you cook dinner each night. That is, if you make the family's favorite enchilada recipe on a Tuesday night, you can simply double or triple it and place the extras into the freezer. For very little extra work, you can easily stock the freezer.

Or you might do a quick freezer session on a Thursday evening after dinner. Maybe when you ran do the store to pick up bread for dinner; you noticed that ground beef was marked down. In an hour, you might be able to brown meat for later spaghetti and taco meals and mix up a batch of meatballs. This does require you to have good ideas in your head for what to do with certain proteins and other ingredients, but if you begin freezer cooking, you will quickly develop a repertoire of favorites.

Even the busiest of people can usually find time to freezer cook; if you decide it's important, you can usually find a way to fit it in.

9. You don't like the recipes.

It's possible (though we think unlikely) that you might read through the entire recipe section of this book and decide that you don't like the looks of any of the recipes. Now what?

You have several options. First, you can figure out how to make your favorite recipes freezer friendly (with the tips we'll provide in a bit). This is your best option, because it ensures that the resulting product is something you and your family will want to eat. Even if you think that your favorite recipes are complicated or not freezer friendly, you might be surprised at how amazingly simple it is to make them friendly for the freezer.

That said, there are 80 recipes in this book. We think you'll find at least a few that suits your needs or your eating preferences. Start with the ones that you are sure you'll like and then move on to recipes that you aren't sure about. You might simply tweak them a bit to make them yours and then they'll be fine. If you still aren't sure, start with the breakfast recipes. Most are simple favorites that freeze well and can be a great introduction to the concept of cooking for the freezer.

10. You have to remember to eat the stuff in the freezer.

This can be a con. Many a freezer cook has done an entire session of freezer recipes only to forget that they have a freezer full of food. Instead, they make a menu plan as usual and do their regular shopping, thus falling into old habits.

The way to deal with this is simple – keep a running list of what you have. Many people will keep a simple list on their refrigerator that tells them what's in the freezer and how much of it there is. As you remove something, simply change the total amount in the freezer or cross it off the list altogether. Simple and easy.

The last thing you want to do is work hard to create all of these dishes for the freezer and then forget they are there. Once you start freezer cooking, therefore, you'll want to come up with some kind of system that helps you keep track of your inventory. What Can You Freeze?

Perhaps the better question here is what you can't freeze. There are few foods that can't be frozen, but in general most foods and dishes are fair game.

As you will see from the recipes in this book, there is a wide array of foods that can be frozen in various states. Let's look at what that means.

- **Complete meals** – You can freeze complete meals, such as enchiladas or pasta casserole dishes. These can even be cooked before being put in the freezer; and then you simply heat and eat. Lasagna is a popular complete meal that people like to keep in the freezer.
- **Components of meals** -- Some meals will need to be frozen in components. One example of this is chicken fajitas (recipe in this book). While you could freeze chicken, peppers and onions that have already been cooked, in general that's not an ideal option. The quality of the reheated food likely won't

be anywhere near what it is fresh. Instead, you can freeze the components. You might freeze the uncooked chicken in marinade as well as a separate bag containing peppers and onions. You can freeze all of this with tortillas and even a bag of shredded cheese. Everything gets thawed and cooked as needed (you can cook the chicken ahead of time if you like).

- **"Dump" meals** – While there aren't too many of these in this book, you can find hundreds of recipes that fit this style of freezer cooking. You likely have many favorite recipes of this kind and they can easily be converted to freezer recipes. These include beef or chicken recipes that you cook in the slow cooker. You simply freeze the raw meat in the sauce or marinade, along with any vegetables, and then simply "dump" the contents of the freezer bag into the slow cooker a few hours before you're ready to eat. The simplicity lies in the fact that while you can thaw everything before cooking, you can also dump the frozen meat and sauce into the slow cooker and cook it.

- **Extras** – This includes things like sauces and fruits. A wide array of foods fit into this category. Let's say your family eats a lot of potato chips, but they get expensive. You find yourself in the store facing a huge display of sale chips. If you could buy 10 bags, you'd save a good deal of money but – while you know your kids eat a lot of chips – you don't think they will eat all of the chips before they expire. What do you do? You can freeze the chips! Just buy them and put them in the freezer in their original bags. They'll be fine for up to 3 months or so.

- Another example is fruit. A lot of people enjoy picking their own fruit but might buy quantities that are more than they can eat before the fruit goes bad. The freezer comes to the rescue here! Let's say you pick a big batch of raspberries and blueberries. Simply clean the fruit, let it dry well, then place it on a cookie sheet until firm. Once firm, transfer to a freezer bag and you can use that fruit for months to come in smoothies, on your morning oatmeal and in cobbler.

Having said all that, however, there are some things you cannot freeze. Below is a list of foods that you can freeze as well as some you should not freeze. Sometimes you can freeze these items when they are in a recipe, but much depends on the recipe and how the food is used. For example, our recipe for Chicken Pot Pie calls for cream, which you cannot generally freeze by itself. But there's only a small amount in the pot pie mixture and it freezes very well in the filling. You just stir after reheating the mix and it's fine.

Some foods you can freeze (that might surprise you):

- **Cheeses --** We have talked about freezing shredded cheese (and a few recipes in this book have shredded cheese as a component or as part of the recipe) but you can freeze blocks of cheese as well. If you have a hard or semi-hard cheese that you'll have to throw out soon, wrap it in plastic wrap and put in a freezer bag. Do know that it will likely be crumbly when it comes out of the freezer, so plan to use it grated in recipes. After freezing, you won't use this cheese on a cracker.

- **Milk** – Many smart and frugal cooks know this tip. You can buy milk and freeze it. Lower fat milks often freeze better than whole milk, but all can be frozen. Buy cartons when they are on sale, open and pour out ½ to 1 cup and then replace the cap. Freeze the milk for up to 2 months. Give it a good shake to restore the milk fats to normal before pouring.

- **Citrus** – If you have lemons or oranges that are going to go bad, juice them and freeze both the juice and the zest or peel. The juice should be frozen in small amounts – say, ice cube size amounts – but can be used in tea and in recipes. Freeze the zest on a cookie sheet until firm and then put it into a freezer bag.

- **Tomato paste** – Surely we aren't the only ones who have opened a can of tomato paste for a recipe and then realized that we only needed one tablespoon and the rest will go bad. If you have also done this, you might be as excited as we were to hear that you can freeze tomato paste. Simply put a small amount (be sure to measure first so you know how much you have) in an ice cube tray and freeze. You can also just put dollops on a baking sheet, freeze until firm and then place them into a freezer bag.

- **Nuts** – Nuts can go rancid fairly quickly, but if you freeze them, they can last for up to a year. If you're a baker (or just a nut fan) you know that nuts can also be expensive. But if you buy nuts in bulk or at a warehouse store, you can save a good deal of money. Buy nuts this way and store them in the freezer in a freezer bag or hard-sided container. Then just remove the amount you need for cooking, baking or snacking.

- **Fresh herbs** – Herbs are another item that can be expensive (if you don't grow them yourself), and herbs can be frozen in two ways. You can freeze the full stems after they are washed, dried and placed on paper towels. Then place in a freezer bag and freeze them. If you want to freeze cut herbs, place them in an ice cube tray, pour water in to cover the herbs and freeze. Once they are frozen, pop them out of the tray and put in a freezer bag. When you need to use them in a dish, just take one or more cubes straight from the freezer and put in the skillet, letting the water cook off.

There are, however, some foods that either shouldn't be frozen or that will suffer quality issues if frozen.

Some foods that you shouldn't freeze:

- **Potatoes** – You can freeze mashed potatoes and some other cooked potato dishes, but don't freeze uncooked potatoes. Not only will they turn an unsightly brown, but they will also change consistency, turning into mush; they simply aren't good.

- **High water content vegetables** – You can certainly freeze peppers and broccoli without problems, but some vegetables are simply not good candidates for freezing. This includes vegetables like lettuces and zucchini. They will turn into a watery mess.

- **Eggs in the shell and some egg dishes** – By "some" egg dishes, we are specifically referring to deviled eggs. Other egg dishes, like quiche and egg casseroles, are usually fine. You should also never freeze eggs in the shell. Once the inside freezes, it can expand and cause the egg to burst. You can, however, freeze egg yolks (outside the egg) with success.

- **Soft cheeses** – These cheeses – which usually have a fairly high water content – can't be frozen with any amount of success. These include cream cheese, soft cheeses (like brie, for example) and cottage cheese.

- **Mayonnaise** – If you really want to take advantage of that sale, get only enough mayo that you can eat before it goes bad, but don't plan on freezing it. It will separate and will never come back together in any edible form.

Do you see the good news here? This list – that of the things that should not be frozen – is shorter than the list of surprising foods that can be frozen. Add to that all the wonderful dishes you can make and freeze, and you can quickly see how freezer cooking is a power to behold.

Tips for Freezer Storage

While this isn't rocket science, there are a few things to keep in mind when you consider freezer storage.

Let's look at the various methods you can use to freeze items.

- **Foil pans** – Some dishes work best in foil pans. These include casseroles and dishes that can be messy when cooked. While these pans aren't the most green (or environmentally friendly) option, they are handy. You can definitely see a time savings when you use foil pans. If you want to feel like you are being friendlier to the environment, buy pans that are made from recycled foil.

- **Freezer bags** – The preferred option for a number of reasons. First, these are completely disposable. Simple remove the frozen food from the bag, throw away the bag and then cook the food. But more than that, they are space saving. You will, of course, discover your personal preference when it comes to storage, but we like that you can freeze just about any dish in these, lay it flat to freeze and enjoy the fact that one entire dinner might take up only 1" thick of freezer space. A few dishes won't work in freezer bags. These will mostly fall into the "formed" casserole category, such as lasagna and things like stuffed pasta shells.

- **Baking dishes** – Many freezer cooks like to use this method for freezer storage. Line a baking dish with foil and place your freezer cooked food inside. You might bake a dish before freezing, or freeze it in the baking dish until solid. Then remove the foil and the food and place in to a freezer bag. Your food is frozen in the right shape for the baking dish, but you retain the use of the dish while the item is in the freezer. When you're ready to cook, pop the food right back into the dish for cooking. Then just throw the foil away and enjoy a simple clean-up job on the baking dish.

- **Plastic or solid-sided containers** – There are many things that should only be frozen in hard-sided containers. This includes sauces, for example. But hard-sided containers do take quite a bit of room in the freezer, so if you are partial to this kind of storage method, make sure you have enough room in your freezer. Many people prefer these kinds of containers because they generally keep the freezer tidier when full of frozen food, but there is the space issue. Many cooks find that the best solution is a mixed solution – that is, they will use some hard-sided containers and some bags. The mix seems to work well, with the cook deciding which container to use for each dish.

- **Foil or freezer paper** – You can certainly go old school and just wrap things in foil or freezer paper. This won't work for all of your freezing needs, of course, but it's a simple option that can be ideal for many freezing needs.

Once you are comfortable with your freezer containers, you will want to consider how to store all these goodies in your freezer. That is, how will you keep everything organized and neat?

The decisions you make about how to organize your freezer stash will depend largely on the kind of freezer you have. That will also dictate the kind of storage containers you use. For example, if you only have a freezer that's attached to your refrigerator, you might choose to freeze as much as you can in freezer bags, but if you have a standalone freezer, you might worry much less about space and freeze things in whatever container works best for you.

Regardless of your freezer vessel, there are some easy options for organization. **These include:**

- Once freezer bags are flat, you can line them up in a box so all you have to do is to thumb through them to find a dish to make.

- You can organize things by protein. If you have a good deal of pork and chicken frozen, for example, you might designate one shelf of the freezer for chicken and another for pork.

- You might utilize small crates that you can buy at a dollar store. Use these for small items, and tag them. One crate, for example, might hold small bags that each has one recipe's worth of scone or muffin mix. Another crate might hold a variety of shredded cheeses in small freezer bags. A third might hold spice mixes or frozen herbs.

Or you might opt for the popular choice that many cooks make to simply throw it all in the freezer and sort through everything when it's time to pull something out. If you choose this option (while somewhat disorganized, this method can also make good use of every crevice of a freezer), make sure you keep an accurate and up-to-date inventory so nothing gets lost if it's hidden behind something else.

Should you buy a freezer?

People often mistakenly believe that in order to successfully freezer cook, they need to have a standalone freezer. While it can certainly be handy for a number of reasons, it's not necessary. Let's look at the pros and cons of having a standalone freezer.

1. **You will have more room**. This is definitely in the "plus" category. You will have a lot of space in which to store food, which allows you to take advantage of store sales, bulk meat purchases and the like. You won't have to avoid a bulk purchase of anything because you are afraid you don't have the storage space for it.

2. **Your energy bill will likely be higher.** If you decide to purchase a standalone freezer, carefully consider the increased cost of energy to run it. In that vein, choose the smallest standalone freezer that will still serve your needs. Depending on the model and style of freezer you choose, you might only see a slight bump in your energy bill, but that increased cost is something to consider.

3. **You might not need the extra space.** Many freezer cooks successfully freeze 30 days' worth of meals in their fridge-top freezer and even have space left over for ice cube trays and a few cartons of ice cream. Often, it's best to freezer cook for a few months and then make a determination about whether or not you need a separate freezer.

4. **A standalone freezer takes a good deal of space.** If you have a garage or other place to put the freezer, you might not consider this a downside, but you must consider that if you buy a standalone freezer, you need space to keep it and it should be near enough to the house that accessing it is easy. If having a standalone freezer means that you are sacrificing home décor or storage space, it might not be worth it.

5. **You can stock up on other things.** If you want to really save money, you might decide to buy flour in bulk and store it in the freezer. Perhaps you have a very large family and you want to be able to buy bread at a discount bread store and keep it for a month. Since bread products are going to take up a fair amount of space in your freezer, you might find that a standalone freezer is necessary. In the end, a standalone freezer could save you a good deal of money if you use it for more than to just store your freezer cooked items.

Only you can decide if purchasing a standalone freezer makes sense. Your personal situation is just that—yours. The best solution, then, is to consider the various pros and cons and make a decision that best fits your situation.

Tips for Freezer Cooking

Having a freezer full of yummy food isn't an accident. It takes planning, hard work and a commitment to keeping that freezer full. To that end, there are a few things you have to consider when you freezer cook. These include planning, planning and planning even more. Truly, if you plan well and follow your plan, you are nearly guaranteed success at this endeavor.

3 things to do before you plan a freezer cooking session.

Before you can even begin your planning session, you will want to know a few things about your upcoming session. These include the types of recipes/session, dietary considerations and time constraints.

1. **Recipes and session**

Before you even start planning, consider what kinds of recipes you want to make and what kind of session you want to have. Let's start with the recipes.

There are more than 80 recipes in this book and you can find hundreds more in a wide array of places. We suggest starting with the recipes in this book that look good to you and that you think your family will enjoy. Enjoy the meals you make and then decide which ones to keep in your repertoire and which you might not make again.

After you have a few recipes to work from, you can begin to collect recipes from other places. Do you have tried and tested family recipes that you would like to keep on hand for days when you don't have time to cook? Can you convert those recipes into freezer recipes? If so, include those recipes in your freezer session.

You might enjoy a special dish at a friend's house and ask for the recipe, but get overwhelmed with the sheer number of ingredients and the prep time required to make it. Think about how you can make that recipe into a freezer cooking recipe. Make the conversions necessary and write out the recipe. You can consider including this in your session.

Aside from choosing you recipes, you will want to choose the kind of session you will have. That is, it's hard to do a baking session and a dinner session on the same day. If you are only making a few recipes of each, you likely can combine these sessions, but many freezer cooks like to focus on a particular kind of session each time they get to work.

Here are some ideas for different sessions you can do:

- Breakfast foods
- Dinner foods (or just a beef, chicken or pork session, for example)
- Breads and baked goods (including mixes for brownies and cakes, as well as frozen cookie balls)
- Side dishes
- Appetizers or foods for entertaining

You don't have to be incredibly rigid, here. You can combine some sessions. While combining a large dinner and baking session might be difficult, you could likely combine a baking and a breakfast session. As you'll see from the recipe section, breakfast foods come together quickly for the freezer, so you can likely share the breakfast prep time with something else. The same goes for side dishes – you can likely combine a side dish session with desserts or even appetizers.

So before you go fully into the planning mode, be sure to consider the kind of session you want to have. Perhaps you want to do some dinner dishes, some breakfast dishes and some desserts. You can do this, but you'll have to be very organized and you'll want to plan well. Look in the next chapter (which features a sample cooking session) and see how you can combine sessions.

2. Dietary restrictions

Think about any specific dietary restrictions you or a family member might be facing. While the vast majority of the recipes in this book are relatively healthy, you might need to make other considerations. You might need to reduce the sodium or the fat or even the calories. Examine each recipe you want to make and think about how you can make it suit your dietary needs. As an example, there is a very simple recipe in this book for Sausage Breakfast Sandwiches.

This recipe has just three ingredients:

- Biscuits from a can
- Turkey breakfast sausage patties
- American cheese

The turkey sausage is a choice that's much better than traditional sausage, but you might want to make changes to this recipe, depending on your dietary needs. Here are some examples of changes you might make:

Biscuits – You might buy low-fat canned biscuits, or you might make your own biscuits so you know where every single ingredient came from. You might decide to substitute sourdough bread, though that certainly makes it something other than a biscuit sandwich.

Turkey sausage – Turkey sausage is the best choice for breakfast sausages, but you might decide to get an organic sausage or you might make your own sausage. Perhaps you'll choose a vegetarian sausage patty in order to keep this recipe vegetarian.

American cheese – You might decide you want to purchase low-fat American cheese for this, or cheese purchased from the store deli. You might decide to keep the cheese off altogether or substitute shredded cheddar or other kinds of cheese.

As you can see, there are many tweaks you can make to suit your needs. You might decide to keep some recipe as is and tweak others for dietary reasons. Before you plan your cooking session, consider these needs first.

3. **Time constraints**

Do you have a full day to give to freezer cooking? If not, consider how much time you have and then work a freezer session into that time. Maybe after looking at your calendar you realize that the only time you have is Friday night after work and until bed. You'd be surprised how much you can fit into that time frame if you are organized and you plan ahead. We'll talk about that shortly. For now, give careful consideration to the time you have available and work with that.

Starting your planning.

So are you ready to get started now? You have made a list of recipes you want to make, decided how to make them work for your needs, made tweaks as you see fit and have designated a time you can cook? If so, you are ready to get started.

Aside from the time you'll spend in the kitchen, one of the biggest jobs of any cooking session is planning the shopping and doing a good enough job that you don't forget anything.

Here are some methods you can use to organize your shopping:

- Use a spreadsheet – Many freezer cooks like to create a spreadsheet that allows them to track how much they need of each ingredient. As they go through each recipe they plan on making, they add that ingredient to the spreadsheet so they quickly have a visual look at exactly what they need to plan their session.

- Use freezer session planning sheets – These are available for download all over the Internet or you can create your own. Simply, these will feature charts that let you track (by hand) the ingredients you need for each recipe. You'll make hash marks or use some other method to indicate you need one more onion or another pepper. Then you can tally up all of the ingredients at the end to determine exactly how many peppers and onions (among other things) you need to purchase.

- Use a simple list – This is probably the most common method of planning a shopping trip for freezer cooking. Use a notebook and write down the ingredients you need for each recipe. It might take several pages, but you'll be able to easily transfer this information to a shopping list before you leave home. Because you might want to shop at several stores for your ingredients (the bag-your-own store, the warehouse store and a regular grocery, for example), you can easily pull off certain list items and place them on the appropriate store list.

Before you go shopping.

Now, though you might have a list that you think is accurate and ready to shop with, you will want to do a few things before you head to the store. You're not completely ready just yet.

1. Check your pantry, freezer and refrigerator. Don't assume you need chicken broth; you might be surprised to find that you have six cans of stock on the shelves of your pantry. The

last thing you want to do is to buy a bunch of groceries you don't really need to do your freezer cooking session.

2. After you make your list, make a beeline for your food storage areas. Do you have the stock you need? Do you already have cans of beans or tomatoes? Don't overlook spices and seasonings, either. Not only might you have something you think you need to purchase, you might also need to purchase more dried herbs or seasonings. Don't assume you have enough.

3. Plan the order you'll do the cooking in. Don't just head into the kitchen with a list of recipes and a bunch of ingredients. You might come out OK with meals made and in the freezer, but doing a freezer session this way is a sure way to get frustrated and to create more work and more mess than you might like.

4. Instead, plan your cooking session. Let's say that you are using just that Friday evening for cooking. You should plan to shop on Tuesday or Wednesday (never shop the same day you plan to cook) and you could use a little time on Thursday evening to chop onions and peppers. You might brown hamburger or chop up chicken. If you do just a little prep before the big cooking session you can save time, energy and it will help you to generate less mess than if you do it all at once.

5. To help you both in the pre-cooking stage and the actual cooking stage, plan out the exact order of your cooking session. Are you cooking chicken, beef and some side dishes? Think about how you can make use of your slow cooker, oven and stovetop all at the same time. Let's say one of the side dishes is double-stuffed baked potatoes. You might start by turning on the oven and putting the potatoes in to bake. While they are baking, you can do all of your chicken dishes, then remove the potatoes, get those ready for the freezer,

and move on to beef. No matter what kind of session you are doing, think about how you can maximize your time, energy and ingredients.

6. Think about where you'll keep your groceries and where you'll do the cooking. Please don't just say "kitchen" because it's not quite that simple, though we wish it were, too. Instead, think first about groceries. You could come home with a huge amount of vegetables, meats and cold ingredients like cheese. Do you currently have enough room in your refrigerator for all the cold ingredients that are coming home with you? If not, do you have an extra refrigerator you can use to store some of the ingredients? Can you clean out your fridge to make room for all the ingredients that are coming?

7. Next, think about where you'll do your cooking session. Some cooks like to set up folding tables around the kitchen and eating area that they use either for an extra prep space or to hold foods that are waiting to be prepped or those that are cooling before being put into the freezer.

8. If you have a large kitchen with a good deal of counter space, you should be OK, but many cooks like to give their kitchen a good clean and purge before a cooking session. Don't do a thorough cleaning, because you'll be making a mess and will have to clean it after you are done, but if you get rid of clutter on the countertops and create space that is ideal for your intended purpose, it will make your cooking session go much smoother.

9. Check and re-check your list. If you transferred items from your master list to lists for each store you'll visit, did you make sure to transfer everything? You will want to make sure that each ingredient made its way onto at least one of your lists. Little is more frustrating than to be in the middle

of a cooking session and realize that a critical ingredient is missing because you forgot to buy it.

10. Don't forget freezer cooking essentials. Be sure to add specific items to your list that will be essential to your cooking session. What items you need will be dictated by what kind of session you want to have and how you decide to store items, but here are some ideas:

- Foil pans in various sizes

- Quart and gallon-size freezer bags

- Heavy duty foil

- Freezer paper

- Waxed paper

- Parchment paper

- Freezer tape (for labeling containers)

- Sharpie (for labeling bags)

- Hard-sided containers (plastic works well and everything from plastic to glass is great)

- Sandwich bags

When you go shopping.

You likely have a favorite grocery store where you do the bulk of your shopping. This store might also have the best prices and produce and meat that you are happy with. But most freezer cooks will utilize several stores when shopping for a session. They might do this to save money or to take advantage of getting the best produce, meat and other items at stores they prefer for these purchases.

For example, you might like the meat and bulk produce at the warehouse store, but don't want the 12 cans of tomatoes you have to buy there. So you think you'll head to a local bag-your-own store for tomatoes, beans and the like. You might also decide to visit your favorite local grocer for other ingredients (as well as things you couldn't find at the other stores).

If you have one store that you prefer, by all means shop there, but be prepared to make at least two stops, as you might find that you can't get every single ingredient at one store.

If you do visit more than one store, be careful of two things:

Don't buy the same thing twice. If you have organized grocery lists, this might not happen, but if you are doing a fairly large session, you might inadvertently purchase an item you have already purchased, or that you will purchase at the next store. Be cognizant of what's on your list and be careful not to overbuy and overspend.

Don't forget anything. If you head into store #1 and find they don't have the kind of beans you are looking for, you need to move that item to your next grocery list, so you can be sure to pick up the beans. Don't assume you'll remember it. After you load your car with groceries, be sure to look at your list and move any items you did not get to another list.

If you are tight on time, you could choose to do the shopping for the non-perishable items one day and the shopping for the perishable items on another day. Just make sure that you are ready to cook within a couple of days of purchasing the perishable items.

When you get home, organize your groceries but don't put everything away. Instead, have a staging area where you know you can find those cans of beans or box of cereal. You'll only want to put non-perishable items, of course, as well as most fruits and some vegetables, but having a designated area for groceries is a great help.

When you're ready to cook.

In the next chapter, we'll go through a fictional cooking session so you can see what it might look like, but for now, think about these things:

- **Be well rested;** it might not sound like it will be hard, but a full freezer cooking session will take a lot out of you, so being rested and physically refreshed will go far during your cooking day or cooking session.

- **Think about food the day of your session.** Dinner can especially confound less experienced freezer cooks. Don't assume that you will cook dinner the night you have spent a day in the kitchen cooking for the freezer. Either plan to eat something you have prepped for the freezer, or order a pizza. Seriously. You'll thank us later.

- **Make sure everything you need is ready to use and clean.** You don't want to spend time cleaning a pan or emptying the dishwasher during your session. Pull out skillets, saucepans, mixing bowls and measuring cups. If you have everything at your fingertips, the process will go much smoother in general.

- **Relax and reward yourself when you're done.** The real reward, of course, is having a freezer full of food that's either quick to fix or ready to heat and eat, but also be prepared to reward yourself on your cooking day, maybe with a movie and a glass of wine or a bubble bath.

Sample Freezer Cooking Session

In this section, we'll provide a sample freezer session, and give you a fictional scenario to watch in action. This should give you a good idea of how you might approach your own freezer session. Pay attention to when Laura goes shopping, how she stores her food and how she organizes her time to make best use of it when preparing several meals at once.

For our fictional session, Laura has decided to do a chicken session, a simple ground beef session and to prepare some breakfast foods for the freezer.

Laura will make:

- 12 Breakfast Burritos
- 2 bags of Baked Oatmeal
- 3 bags of dry mix for Chocolate Chip Scones
- 1 bag of Meatballs
- 2 containers of filling for Bierrocks
- 3 bags of cooked hamburger
- 2 bags of components for Chicken Fajitas
- 2 batches of Chicken Divan
- 1 bag of Maple-Glazed Chicken
- 2 uncooked chickens made for Sticky Chicken
- 3 bags of cooked chicken

Laura has decided she only has a few hours to give to this session. She'll cook from the moment she gets up Saturday until about 1 p.m. This is an ambitious plan, but it can be done.

Shopping:

Laura goes shopping Friday evening after work. She heads to a warehouse store and gets her meat and some produce (such as onions). She picks up the rest of the groceries at her local grocery store closer to home.

At home, she puts all the perishable items in the refrigerator and non-perishables on her dining room table. She does no pre-prep that night.

On Saturday:

Laura starts at 7 a.m. She decides to start with the breakfast items so she can get those in the freezer before working on the meats.

To that end, she starts by laying her bacon on a baking sheet and baking it in a 400-degree oven while she works on other things. She scrambles eggs and grates cheese. She browns the hash browns. Once the bacon is done, she lets it cool and then crumbles it. Just before the bacon was ready, she put the tortillas in the oven for 5 minutes to make them warm and pliable.

Laura puts the burritos together and gets them into freezer bags. Those bags are put on a side table for the time being. The pans are put in the sink to wash later.

Now Laura puts together the baked oatmeal and scones, spending a total of 15 minutes putting it all together.

Laura sets a timer for 10 minutes and speed cleans the kitchen, making sure to get all the measuring cups and skillets clean, and wiping down countertops.

Now ready to move onto the beef, Laura chops the onions for the bierrocks and the meatballs. While she's doing that, she browns several pounds of hamburger. She removes half of it and creates the bierrocks mix in the skillet with the leftover meat. She doesn't have time to make dough, so she freezes the mix by itself and will make either fresh dough before making the bierrocks or she'll use frozen bread dough.

The rest of the cooked hamburger is placed into small freezer bags. They are labeled for tacos and spaghetti. The small bags are placed into a larger freezer bag and put into the freezer.

To finish off the beef session, Laura mixes up the meatballs and places the meatballs on a cookie sheet to freeze before they get put in a freezer bag.

Laura does a quick clean again, this time focusing on cutting boards, knives and wiping the kitchen down. She places five pounds of chicken breasts in a large stock pot and covers the chicken with water, salt and pepper and brings it to a boil.

While the chicken is cooking, Laura prepares two chickens for sticky chicken and puts the maple-glazed chicken together. Those go in the freezer. When the chicken is cooked, it gets drained and set aside to cool. She puts together bags for chicken fajitas. Then she makes chicken divan with half of the cooked chicken.

The rest of the cooked chicken is divided up and placed in small freezer bags for later use in quesadillas, chicken noodle soup and salads.

Laura removes the meatballs from the freezer and puts them in a large freezer bag and into the freezer.

Laura spends 30 minutes washing dishes, cleaning off countertops and mopping floors. While she's tired, she's also exhilarated because in a short period of time, she has prepared enough food for 24 meals.

Tools

While there's no need to invest in expensive equipment to freezer cook, there are some things that can make the job much easier. These include:

- **A cookie scoop** – Use to make cookie balls for the freezer, as well as to make meatballs.

- **Good knives** – Sharpen your knives or buy a new set, but make sure you have a serviceable set of knives that can handle a variety of cutting jobs from onions to raw meat.

- **A garlic press** – Makes easy work of mincing garlic (you can use these for ginger, too).

- **A variety of mixing bowls** – If you don't often use mixing bowls, you might not have a good set, but having several mixing bowls in several sizes can save you a lot of hand washing.

- **A half-sheet baking pan** – These pans are smaller than traditional cookie sheets and are ideal for freezing berries and meatballs as well as other items before putting them into freezer bags. The smaller size makes them ideal for most freezers, especially smaller freezers.

- **Good containers** – If you decide to freezer cook often, you might want to invest in good hard-sided containers. Glass is not recommended because when frozen, these containers can break easily if dropped, but good quality BPA-free plastic is ideal. Less expensive, "throwaway" containers will also work well.

- **A pastry bag and large tip** – These can be useful for filling potato halves for double-stuffed baked potatoes and for filling cheese-stuffed shells with a minimum of mess.

Tips & Tricks

Freeze it once

Don't re-freeze meats. If you buy a lot of meat during a great sale and can't deal with it right then, feel free to throw it in the freezer. You can use it in a later freezer session. But the meat must be COOKED before you put it back in the freezer the second time. You can't re-freeze uncooked meat and you can't re-freeze cooked meat. (So, by the same token, if you thaw out cooked meat, don't re-freeze it even if it is put into a specific recipe.)

Patience, child

Stagger how you put things in the freezer. That is, don't put a lot of hot food in the freezer at once. Nearly every recipe in this book will say to "cool" and then freeze the dish. This ensures that you keep the temperature of your freezer accurate; if you put too much hot food in the freezer at once, you will tax the freezer and cause it to increase its internal temperature. Not only will it take longer for your food to freeze, but items that are in the freezer already could suffer as well.

Convert and customize

If you learn how to convert your favorite recipes to freezer recipes, you can create a freezer full of food you know you will love because it's full of favorite dishes that you have frozen.

Here's a random example of a family favorite you might want to convert:

Chicken Cacciatore

- Chicken cacciatore recipes usually require you to brown the chicken, and then remove it while you cook vegetables in the same pan. The chicken is added back to the pan with wine and tomatoes and the whole thing is cooked until the chicken is done.

- To convert this recipe (which most people likely think needs to be made fresh), you would brown the chicken, remove it from the pan and then make the sauce. Continue cooking until the moment when the chicken is added back to the pan. This where you freeze it. You would put the chicken in a freezer bag, pour the sauce over and freeze.

- When you're ready to eat, you simply thaw the chicken overnight, pour the contents of the bag into a deep skillet and continue on with the recipe. Cook the pasta fresh; don't freeze this.

Let's say you enjoy tacos each Friday night. You might think there's little you can do to get ahead of this relatively simple meal. Wrong! In this case, you can simply **make taco kits.**

- Buy your tortillas from the warehouse store and divide them up into meal-sized portions. Put them in freezer bags. Cook meat and season it, then portion it out and also put in freezer bags. You can even put the grated cheese in freezer bags. If you make homemade refried beans and freeze them (recipe in this book) you can package them up as well.

- Now, in a large freezer bag, place a bag of meat, a bag of refried beans, a package of tortillas and a bag of cheese. When it's taco night, just thaw everything out, heat the meat and beans, make the tortillas into taco shells and add fresh ingredients like lettuce, tomato, onion and sour cream.

- By purchasing the taco items in bulk, you can make an inexpensive meal even cheaper and you have also made it even simpler.

Working within the budget

If you are motivated to start freezer cooking because you need to save money, you might wonder how you can get started since you will have to spend a lot of money on groceries all at once. You have a few options to get started:

1. Figure out the kinds of freezer meals you want to make and then slowly acquire the ingredients for them. For example, if tomatoes and chicken broth are on a good sale one week, you might buy several cans of each, absorbing the extra cost into your food budget. After a few weeks, you'll likely have enough groceries to get started.

2. You can earmark some extra cash for freezer cooking. You'll only have to get started once, so if you have a block of cash coming (say, from a tax return, work bonus, or garage sale) earmark that money for your first freezer grocery store run.

3. Save the cash. Work on saving money on groceries for a few weeks and take the savings and add it to your freezer cooking stash. After a few weeks, you'll have enough money to get started.

4. Do a small freezer cooking session. Plan a week's worth of meals for your freezer session or do just a breakfast or lunch session. As you save money from having made those meals, you'll be able to transfer money into a dinner or a big session.

Test first

If you have never made a recipe before, don't make a huge batch and plan to eat off it for several meals. If you don't like the recipe, you're stuck with several more meals of it. At most, make two meals of a recipe. If you don't like it, you'll have only one more meal to endure before you can cut it out permanently from future freezer cooking sessions.

Ideally, you should only freeze meals you have tried before. If it's a new recipe, you could make enough for just one meal and eat it one night for dinner. If it's a hit, you can add the full recipe to your next freezer cooking session.

Take advantage of your extra time

One of the great advantages of freezer cooking is all the time it gives you back. If you dislike cooking, it ensures you only have to do it now and then (for the freezer session). If you enjoy cooking, you can still add some cooking days each month to your agenda.

But one other thing freezer cooking gives you is an opportunity to enjoy cooking a bit more. That is, if you can pull an entrée out of the freezer, you might have time to make that great bread you wanted to try, or the more complicated side dish you wouldn't normally have time for. On a night when your entrée is in the oven (and for which you didn't need to mix or measure anything) you can spend time making a fresh dessert and surprise the family.

On the flip side, if you enjoy making the entrée, but tend to dislike fleshing out the meal with sides, bread and dessert, you can focus your freezer sessions on side dishes and simply pull those out of the freezer while you take time making the main dish. The flexibility is limitless.

Take time to plan

If you get excited to do a freezer session, it can be tempting to jump right in. You'll do a freezer session this weekend! You could do one immediately, but don't forget the necessary planning you need in order to have a successful session. You need to:

- Find the right recipes

- Make a thorough shopping list

- Research what you already have in the pantry

- Go shopping (a big job)

- Prepare the kitchen for the session

There is a fair amount of work involved before you even start cooking. Don't get so excited by the whole thing that you forget the necessary steps. If you shop tonight, for example, and begin cooking tomorrow morning, you might discover that you didn't shop well and are missing ingredients, or regret not straightening up the kitchen first.

If you don't take time to do it right, you might decide that freezer cooking is too hard and you won't do it, which would be a shame.

Share the load

If you think that a freezer session might be overwhelming for you or you have a small family and don't need multiples of recipes, consider sharing the load with a friend. You and a friend can plan a freezer session together and share the dishes once you are done. There are many advantages to this plan:

- You can save money

- You can share the work, dishes and mess cleanup

- You can benefit by getting a variety of freezer dishes that you might not have if you do a session on your own

- You can spend some fun time with a friend

If you and your friend can't coordinate a time to shop and cook together, you can each do a freezer session and then share the goodies. For example, you might make two chicken pot pies, three bags of chicken and two dozen cookie balls. You might share a chicken pot pie, a bag of chicken and a dozen cookie balls. In return, you might receive beef stew, chocolate muffins and breakfast burritos.

Get the air out

When you seal your packages up for the freezer, do everything you can do get all the air out. This will keep your frozen food fresh longer and help to prevent freezer burn or ice crystals forming on the food.

When using freezer bags, there are two methods that work best:

The straw method – Simply seal the package up nearly to a corner and then insert a straw into the bag. Such out as much air as you can and seal the bag quickly.

The flatten-it method – When you are sealing your bags for the freezer, simply lean into them and try to get as much air out as you can, flattening the bag as you go. It's not quite as effective as the straw method but works in a pinch.

Work with your kitchen

If you have an apartment kitchen or an old kitchen or a kitchen that just poses a challenge for some reason, don't fight against it. Work with what you have. If you have a very small kitchen, for example, do smaller sessions or put up temporary tables when you're doing a freezer session so you have plenty of "counter" space.

People have freezer cooked in everything from trailers to tiny studio apartments. If you are committed to making it work, you can make it work. The key is to work with what you have. Don't make excuses for it – work through it.

If you really can't cook in your kitchen for whatever reason, but you are committed to doing a freezer session, look into other options. You might ask someone if you can borrow their kitchen for a day. You might leave them a yummy meal in the freezer as payment. You could borrow a church kitchen or rent a kitchen somewhere.

This of this: If your kitchen is really limited and creates real problems for you when cooking, freezer cooking actually helps you because you'll only have to really work in it long enough to do a freezer session and after, you'll only have to reheat and eat.

Don't overlook alternative sources for groceries

As you become an expert at freezer cooking, you'll surely discover a wide array of favorite recipes. Maybe some ingredients are hard to find or expensive. When you are regularly freezer cooking, you can take advantage of bulk purchases as well as alternative sources for your groceries. These might include:

- Farmer's markets
- Online bulk purchases
- Farm share boxes
- Purchases of whole or half cows or pigs

When you begin to use alternative sources of groceries, you can often greatly increase the quality of your food as well as decrease your costs.

Be flexible

This book does not specifically give you a 30-day freezer meal planner (or a 2-week planner), because it focuses on the recipes and gives you the option to pick and choose which recipes you want to use in your freezer session.

Many books do push the concept of cooking 30 days' worth of meals in one day. It's certainly a lofty goal and – if you are successful at it – cooking for 30 days can give quite a bit of convenience.

Your needs, however, might dictate that you cook more or fewer meals. If you have time to make 30 meals and that's how you want to proceed, by all means do it, but don't feel as if you are required to cook this way.

If you want to cook every two weeks, do that. Some cooks find that they prefer doing mini sessions, creating sessions on the fly when they find a good deal on meat or a specific vegetable (like potatoes).

Think about your schedule, your needs and your preferences and create a cooking session that works for all of those things.

Safeguard against leaks

If you freeze your food in freezer bags, it's best to use two bags. That way you reduce the chance that the contents will leak all over your refrigerator while thawing. You might also put a plate or platter under the bag to prevent leaks.

How to Use This Book

What follows are more than 80 recipes that run the gamut from peanut butter and jelly sandwiches to hummus and sweet and sour chicken. There is literally something for everyone.

Here are some suggestions and tips for how to use this book:

1. Pick the recipes that you want to include in your cooking session, paying attention to repeat ingredients. The more repeat ingredients you have, the easier your shopping will be and the more money you'll save.

2. Plan your cooking session, following the tips found in the "Tips for Freezer Cooking" chapter.

3. Prepare the recipe according to the directions. Or, if you have dietary restrictions, make changes as necessary, but make sure those changes won't dramatically change the freezer-friendly nature of the recipe.

4. Label everything. You can do this with freezer tape or by writing directly on the freezer bag. While reheating instructions are included with each recipe, it can save a great deal of time to put the cooking or heating instructions on the bag or container so you can see at a glance what to do in order to get that dish on the table.

5. The majority of the recipes say to "thaw overnight" in the refrigerator, but you have other options. Thawing in the refrigerator is ideal because it allows the food to thaw at a natural and healthy pace, but you can microwave food until it's just thawed or sometimes cook from frozen (but that option will usually be noted in the recipe).

6. Most recipes refer to putting the freezer food in a freezer bag. Freezer bags can be great because they are space saving, inexpensive and disposable. But not everyone wants

to use freezer bags for their freezer food. You can use any option you choose for most dishes. You might prefer using hard-sided containers, foil pans or a baking dish. There are times when a bag is most appropriate, but you can make that determination.

7. If you want to cook the recipes that are the healthiest, here is a list of the healthiest recipes in the book:

a. Moo Shu Pork

b. Pork tenderloin in orange sauce

c. Hummus

d. Beef with broccoli

e. Freezer Cole slaw

f. Chicken and noodle soup

g. Creamy carrot soup with dill

h. Lentil soup

i. Baked oatmeal

j. Very berry fruit smoothie

k. Chicken fajitas

l. Tex Mex chicken and beans

m. Applesauce

n. Busy bananas

8. Looking for recipes that won't break the bank? These (and others) can all be prepared for under $5 a meal.

a. Bierrocks

b. Garlic beef enchiladas

c. Greek chicken and rice

d. Sticky chicken

e. Sausage tacos

f. Minestrone

g. Vegetable chowder

9. Want to keep some things on hand for on-the-fly entertaining? Try the following:

a. Hot pizza dip

b. Jalapeno poppers

c. Pizza kits

d. Strawberry granita

e. Black and white cheesecake bars

Let's get cooking!

Breakfast

People often don't think about breakfast foods when planning a freezer session, and that's a mistake; breakfast foods are some of the most freezer-friendly. Consider how your favorite recipes can be converted to freezer recipes and use some of the tried and true favorites in this chapter for convenient breakfasts every day of the week.

Baked Oatmeal

Serves 4.

Method: Mix oatmeal, freeze, and bake when ready to eat.

Ingredients:

- 3 tab. butter, melted
- 1 large egg
- 1/3 c. sugar
- ¾ teas. baking powder
- ¾ teas. vanilla
- ½ teas. cinnamon
- Pinch salt
- ½ c. milk
- 1 ½ c. oats

To prepare for the freezer: Beat the egg, sugar and butter together. Mix in the rest of the ingredients except milk and oats. Stir in oats and milk by hand and stir just until blended. Pour mixture into a freezer bag. Freeze.

When you're ready to eat: Thaw the bag of oatmeal overnight in the refrigerator. In the morning, heat oven to 350 degrees and pour mixture into a baking pan sprayed with cooking spray. Bake for about 20 to 30 minutes or until the oatmeal is set in the middle. Serve warm with milk; add brown sugar if you like a sweeter oatmeal. You can top this with fresh fruit, like blueberries, if you like.

Breakfast Burritos

Makes 12.

Method: Prepare and freeze to reheat before eating.

Ingredients:

- 12 flour tortillas
- 12 eggs
- Salt
- Pepper
- 2-3 tab. milk
- 4 ounces grated cheddar (or preferred kind) cheese
- ½ bag of frozen hash brown potatoes
- 2 tab. vegetable oil
- 6 slices bacon
- Salsa (optional)

To prepare for the freezer: Scramble eggs with a dash of milk (or roughly 2-3 tablespoons of milk); add salt and pepper to taste. Cook eggs in a large skillet over medium heat until done. Remove from pan, wipe out and cook bacon until crisp. When bacon is cool, crumble into small pieces and mix into eggs.

Meanwhile, in another large skillet, heat oil until hot and then add potatoes. Cook until potatoes are heated through and slightly crispy. Season with salt and pepper if desired. Let cool.

On each tortilla, layer eggs, potatoes and a small amount of cheese. Add a teaspoon of salsa, if desired. Roll each burrito and wrap in foil. Place in freezer bag.

When you're ready to eat: Reheat burrito in oven at 350 degrees for about 30 minutes or until heated through. To heat in microwave, unwrap burrito from foil and wrap in a paper towel. Cook for 1 ½ minutes or until hot.

Chocolate Chip Scones

Some scones are soft like cake, while others are more biscuit like in texture and style. These are the latter. The oats make them a bit more substantial than a typical scone.

Makes 8 scones.

Method: Freeze dry mix and bake when ready to eat.

Ingredients:

- 1 ½ c. all-purpose flour
- 1 c. oats
- ¼ c. sugar
- 1 ½ teas. baking powder
- ½ teas. salt
- ¼ c. butter
- ½ c. chocolate chips

To have on serving day:

- 2/3 c. buttermilk

- Sugar

To prepare for the freezer: Combine the flour, oats, sugar, baking powder and salt. Cut the butter into the mixture using two forks or a pastry cutter. Once the butter is mixed (it should be the size of peas), add the chocolate chips, put mixture into a quart-sized freezer bag, and freeze.

When you're ready to eat: Pull bag out of the freezer (no need to thaw first) and preheat oven to 400 degrees. Dump dry ingredients into a bowl and add the buttermilk. Stir until just mixed. Line a baking sheet with parchment paper and dump the contents of the bowl on to the baking sheet. Carefully form the mixture into a round disc about 1-inch thick. Cut into 8 pieces. Sprinkle with sugar and bake for about 15 minutes or until brown.

Note: You can prepare the scones all the way through the baking and then freeze, wrapped in wax paper, until ready to eat. Warm in the microwave or oven.

Apple Buttermilk Muffins

Muffins are some of the friendliest of all freezer-friendly foods. This recipe is a tried and true delicious favorite, but you can make just about any kind of muffin and turn it into a freezer recipe. Most can be baked and then frozen; simply thaw and enjoy.

Makes 12 muffins.

Method: Bake muffins and freeze. Thaw when ready to eat.

Ingredients:

- 2 c. all-purpose flour
- ½ c. light brown sugar, packed
- 2 teas. baking powder
- 1 teas. baking soda
- ½ teas. salt
- 1 c. low-fat buttermilk
- ¼ c. canola oil
- 2 teas. vanilla
- 1 large egg
- 2 medium-size apples (Golden Delicious or Gala work well) peeled, cored and diced
- ½ c. chopped walnuts (optional)
- Topping:

- 1 ½ teas. sugar
- ½ teas. ground cinnamon

To prepare for the freezer: Grease muffin tin or line with paper liners. Preheat oven to 400 degrees.

In a large bowl, mix the dry ingredients. In a small bowl, beat the buttermilk, oil, vanilla and egg with a fork or whisk until mixed. Stir into flour mixture until just mixed (batter will be lumpy). Don't over mix. Fold in the apples and nuts, if using.

Spoon the batter into the muffin cups. In a small bowl, mix the sugar and cinnamon. Sprinkle the tops of the muffins with the cinnamon sugar.

Bake muffins for approximately 20 minutes or until a toothpick inserted into the center of a muffin comes out clean. Remove from the muffin tin and let cool completely. Place in freezer bags.

When you're ready to eat: Thaw on counter and enjoy, or place in microwave in 1-minute intervals until hot.

Breakfast Sandwiches

If you are tempted by the allure of the golden arches in the mornings, make these in bulk and keep them on hand. You'll save money, fat and calories. Like everything else you put up in the freezer, you can control ingredients (for example, you might choose to make these only with egg whites).

Makes 16 breakfast sandwiches.

Method: Put together and freeze. Microwave (or heat in oven) when ready to eat.

Ingredients**:**

- 16 English muffins
- 16 slices Canadian bacon
- 24 eggs
- 2 tab. milk
- 16 slices American Cheese
- Salt

- Pepper

To prepare for the freezer: Break eggs into bowl and whisk with milk. Add salt and pepper to taste. Place a large skillet over medium heat and cook eggs until they are scrambled the way you like them. Split the English muffins.

On one half of each English muffin place an egg, a piece of cheese and a slice of Canadian bacon. Top with other half of muffin. Wrap in foil. Do this for all 16 sandwiches. Place in freezer bag.

When you're ready to eat: You can heat these in the microwave or oven. To heat in the microwave from frozen, unwrap foil and wrap sandwich in a paper towel. Microwave for 1 ½ minutes; turn over, and microwave for 1 minute more or until hot.

To heat in the oven, place the foil-wrapped sandwich in a 350-degree oven and heat until hot, about 30 minutes.

Sausage Breakfast Sandwiches

These are a cinch to make, yet replicate well the popular sausage biscuit sandwiches sold in some fast food restaurants.

Makes 8 sandwiches.

Method: Make these and freeze, then reheat when ready to eat.

Ingredients:

- 1 can (containing 8) biscuits
- 1 box (containing 8) turkey sausage patties
- 4 slices American cheese

To prepare for the freezer: Bake biscuits according to directions on package. When brown, remove from oven and let cool.

Meanwhile, brown turkey sausage in a skillet until brown and heated through. Tear each piece of American cheese in half so you have a total of 8 pieces of cheese.

Assemble the sandwiches by splitting a biscuit in half and placing one sausage patty and one piece of cheese on one half. Replace second half of biscuit and wrap biscuit sandwiches in foil.

When you're ready to eat: Remove desired number of sandwiches from freezer and place in a 350-degree oven, heating until hot (about 25 minutes). If desired, heat in microwave by removing the sandwiches from the foil and wrapping them in paper towels. Heat for 1 minute, turn over and heat 1 minute more, or until heated through.

Simple Pancakes

With this recipe, you can create two quart-sized bags of pancake mix for simple weekday morning breakfasts. Of course, you can also cook your pancakes and freeze them for an easier preparation method. Many people, however, aren't fond of reheated pancakes. You can always try both methods to see which one works best for you.

Each bag of pancake mix will make 8 to 10 regular-sized pancakes.

Method: Freeze bags of dry mix and add wet ingredients before cooking.

Ingredients:

- 2 cups all-purpose flour
- 2 tab. Su gar
- 3 ½ teas. baking powder
- ½ teas. salt

To have on serving day (for each bag):

1 egg, beaten

1 cup milk

2 tablespoons cooking oil

To prepare for the freezer: Mix all dry ingredients, whisking until the mixture is finely mixed. Mark two quart-sized freezer bags with "Pancakes" and place half of the mixture into each of two bags. Freeze.

When you're ready to eat: You can use the mix straight out of the freezer, or pull out an hour (or a day) before using. Empty contents of bag into a large bowl and add the egg, milk and oil. Mix well.

Pour about ¼ cup of batter onto a hot, lightly greased griddle or fry pan. Cook until each pancake is golden brown.

(To make blueberry pancakes, simply scatter a small handful of blueberries on the pancakes while they are in the pan and before you turn them over; you can use fresh or frozen blueberries.)

Streusel Topped Banana Bread

This bread is sweet and rich. It's a great bread to gift to friends and family and it freezes well.

Makes 10 servings.

Method: Bake bread and freeze. Thaw when ready to eat.

Ingredients:

- ½ c. vegetable shortening
- ¾ c. sugar
- 1 large egg
- 4 teas. lemon juice
- 2 c. flour
- 1 teas. baking soda
- ½ teas. salt
- 1 ½ c. mashed banana (2-4 very ripe bananas)
- 1 c. walnuts

For streusel:

- ½ c. flour
- ½ c. packed brown sugar
- ¼ c. butter, softened
- ½ teas. nutmeg

- ½ teas. cinnamon

To prepare for the freezer: Preheat oven to 350 degrees. Cream together the shortening and sugar until well blended and smooth. Beat in the egg and lemon juice. Add flour, baking soda, and salt. Fold the mixture into the batter and blend well. Stir in the mashed banana and walnuts. Pour the mixture into a loaf pan.

To make the streusel, mix all streusel ingredients in a bowl with a fork until crumbly. Sprinkle over the banana bread and bake the bread for about 50 to 55 minutes or until a toothpick comes out clean. Let cool.

Once cool, wrap bread in plastic wrap and place in a freezer bag.

When you're ready to eat: Let bread thaw on countertop for about 2 hours or until thawed.

Very Berry Fruit Smoothie

Fruit smoothies freeze well in small containers, like mason jars. If you find the plastic jars, they work even better. You can use a wide array of ingredients in smoothies, of course, but this recipe creates a sweet berry smoothie that's also high in nutrients.

Makes 2 large or 4 small glasses of smoothie.

Method: Mix in blender, freeze for later drinking.

Ingredients:

- 1 banana
- 1 ½ cups frozen berries
- 1 cup Greek vanilla yogurt
- 1 tablespoon honey
- 1 cup grape, orange or apple juice
- 1 scoop vanilla protein powder
- 1 tablespoon flax meal

To prepare for the freezer: Put ingredients into blender in the order listed. Blend until a smooth, drinkable consistency. Add more juice if you like a thinner smoothie. Pour into plastic or glass mason jars (4 ounce size) and freeze, or pour into 2 8-ounce mason jars.

When you're ready to drink: Thaw overnight in the refrigerator or for an hour or so on the kitchen countertop. Stir to mix the liquids and solids together, and enjoy.

Cinnamon Chip Scones

Those who like cinnamon will love these scones. They are rich, flavorful, and a cinch to make when you prep ahead and put the dry mix in the freezer.

Serves 8 (1 scone each).

Method: Mix dry ingredients together, cut in butter and chips and freeze so these can be made quickly at a later date.

Ingredients:

- 2 c. flour
- 2 teas. baking powder
- ½ teas. baking soda
- ½ teas. salt
- ½ cup cold butter
- ½ c. cinnamon chips

To have on serving day:

- 1 egg
- 3 tablespoons honey
- 1/3 c. buttermilk
- 2 tab. sugar

To prepare for the freezer: Whisk together the flour, baking powder, baking soda and salt. Cut in butter with two forks or a pastry blender until it's the size of peas. Stir in cinnamon chips. Place mixture in quart-sized freezer bags and freeze.

When you're ready to eat: Separate egg; save white for another use. Dump frozen mixture into a bowl and add the egg, honey and buttermilk. Mix well, but don't over mix. Mix will be slightly crumbly. Pour mixture out onto a baking sheet lined with parchment paper and pat it into a circle about 1/2" thick. Cut into 8 wedges, sprinkle with sugar, and bake at 400 degrees for about 15 to 20 minutes or until brown.

You can drizzle a glaze over these if you want to once they are baked. Simply mix together ½ c. powdered sugar, 1-2 teaspoons of milk and ¼ teas. vanilla; drizzle over hot scones.

Note: If you like, you can bake these before freezing them. When cool, wrap in waxed paper and freeze. Thaw and reheat to eat.

Note: Cinnamon chips are available in the fall and through the holidays in stores. You can usually buy them online throughout the year. If you can't find the chips, make recipe as directed, but add ½ teaspoon cinnamon to the sugar you sprinkle on the top of the scones. This will impart a similar cinnamon flavor.

Appetizers

Appetizers can take time to make, but when it's party time, you might not have the time or energy to make them. Keep some on hand in the freezer so you only have to pull them out when you need them. You'll quickly figure out how to make your favorite appetizer recipes freezer-friendly.

Hot Pizza Dip

Makes 12 servings.

Method: Make and bake dip, cooking for additional time before serving.

Ingredients:

- 8 oz. cream cheese, softened
- 4 oz. sour cream
- 1/8 teas. garlic powder
- ¼ teas. dried oregano

- ¾ c. store-bought pizza sauce
- ½ c. pepperoni, diced
- ¼ c. onion, chopped (optional)
- ¼ c. green peppers, diced (optional)

To have on serving day:

- 1 c. mozzarella cheese
- Tortilla chips

To prepare for the freezer: In a medium bowl, combine cream cheese, sour cream, garlic powder and oregano. Spread the mixture into a 9" foil cake pan.

Spread the pizza sauce over the cream cheese mixture. Sprinkle the pepperoni over and sprinkle green pepper and onion, if using. Bake at 350 for 15 to 20 minutes or until hot. Let cool.

When cool, cover the top of the dip with foil or plastic wrap and place the pan into a large freezer bag.

When you're ready to eat: Thaw the dip overnight in the refrigerator. Preheat oven to 350 degrees and put the dip in the oven. Remove from oven, sprinkle the mozzarella cheese over, and return to oven for about 8 to 10 minutes or until hot and cheese is melted. Use tortilla chips to dip.

Note: You can dip other things in this dip, such as breadsticks, vegetables and crackers.

Bbq Chicken Wings

These are easy to make and keep in the freezer for when the snack mood hits. Double or triple recipe as needed.

Makes 16.

Method: Season, partially bake and freeze in sauce. Bake when ready to eat.

Ingredients:

- 1 ½ lb. chicken wings (about 8 wings)
- ½ c. ketchup
- ¼ c. finely chopped onion
- 1 tab. honey
- 1 tab. white vinegar
- 1 clove garlic, minced

To prepare for the freezer: Pat the chicken dry. Cut off and discard the wing tips. Cut each of the wings at the joint to make 2 sections. Place in a single layer on a rimmed baking sheet or 13" x 9" pan. Bake at 375 for about 20 minutes. Drain the fat. Place wings in a freezer bag.

In a small bowl, combine all remaining ingredients. Pour over wings in bag and freeze.

When you're ready to eat: Thaw bag overnight in refrigerator. Preheat oven to 375 degrees. Pour sauce into a small saucepan and heat, until boiling, for about 3 to 5 minutes. Place wings on baking sheet and bake, basting with the sauce every 5 to 10 minutes. Bake for about 20 minutes total, or until wings are tender and cooked through.

Baked Mozzarella Bites

These taste a lot like the deep-fried mozzarella sticks, but they are baked instead of fried. Freeze them unbaked and then bake them when you want to eat them.

Makes 64 bites.

Method: Freeze unbaked and bake when you need them.

Ingredients:

- 16 mozzarella sticks, cut into 4 pieces each
- 2 eggs
- 1 tab. water
- 1 c. Italian seasoned bread crumbs
- 3 tab. flour
- To have on serving day:
- 1 c. spaghetti sauce, warmed

To prepare for the freezer: In a small bowl, beat the eggs and water. Place the bread crumbs in a large plastic bag. Place the flour in a small dish.

Dip the mozzarella bites into the flour, then the eggs. Finally, place them in the bag with the bread crumbs and shake well so they are coated well.

Place the bites on a cookie sheet lined with waxed paper or parchment paper. Freeze. When solid, place them into large freezer bags.

When you're ready to eat: Preheat oven to 400 degrees. Place the desired number of bites on an ungreased baking sheet and bake for 5 to 8 minutes or until thoroughly heated. Allow the bites to sit for a minute before serving. Serve with warmed spaghetti sauce.

Jalapeno Poppers

One of the most popular of all appetizers, these freeze well. Keep plenty on hand because these get gobbled up!

Makes 30.

Method: Prepare poppers and freeze, cooking just before serving.

Ingredients:

- 12 oz. (1 ½ blocks) cream cheese, softened
- 8 oz. cheddar cheese, shredded
- 2 tab. bacon, cooked and crumbled (about 2 -3 slices)
- 15 jalapeno peppers, cleaned and halved
- 1 c. milk
- 1 c. all-purpose flour
- 1 c. plain bread crumbs

To have on serving day:

- Oil, if frying

To prepare for the freezer: In a small bowl, mix the cream cheese, cheddar cheese and bacon. Carefully spoon this mixture into the jalapeno halves.

Put the milk in one bowl, the flour into another and the bread crumbs in a third. Dip the jalapenos in the milk and then into the flour; make sure they are well coated. Place the coated jalapenos on paper towels to dry for about 10 minutes.

Once the jalapenos are dry, dip them again in milk and then roll in breadcrumbs. Allow these to dry for about 10 minutes and then repeat, making sure the jalapenos are well coated in bread crumbs.

At this point, flash freeze the poppers. Place them on a waxed paper or parchment paper -covered baking sheet and freeze them until solid. Once frozen, transfer them to a freezer bag and put them in the freezer.

When you're ready to eat: You can fry these in hot oil for about 2 to 5 minutes each, or until golden. You can fry them from frozen. Or place in a 400-degree oven for about 30 to 45 minutes or until brown and heated through.

Hummus

Hummus freezes well; simply stir well when thawed.

Makes about 3 cups.

Method: Prepare and freeze. Eat when thawed.

Ingredients:

- 2 cloves garlic, minced
- 2 (15 oz.) cans garbanzo beans, drained and rinse
- 2/3 c. roasted tahini
- 1/3 c. lemon juice (freshly squeezed preferred)
- ¼ to ½ c. water
- ¼ c. olive oil
- ½ teas. salt

To prepare for the freezer: Combine the garlic, beans, tahini, lemon juice, ¼ c. water and olive oil in a food processor. Process until smooth. Starting at ½ teaspoon, add salt to taste. Add more water if necessary to get the mixture to the right texture.

You can freeze hummus in a plastic container. Use several small ones if you won't eat all this hummus at once.

When you're ready to eat: Thaw on countertop. When thawed, stir well to get it to the right consistency. Serve with pita bread or chips, vegetables or crackers.

Sausage Wonton Cups

These appetizers freeze well for up to 3 months and are great to keep on hand not just for parties, but also for casual nights at home.

Makes 16 wonton cups.
Method: Freeze, bake, and heat when ready to eat.

Ingredients:

- 16 wonton wrappers
- 1 ½ lb. pork sausage (mild or hot)
- 4 oz. cream cheese
- 4 oz. cheddar cheese, shredded

To prepare for the freezer: Line muffin cups with the wonton wrappers, shaping the wonton wrappers so they fit well into the cups. You can either use 2 muffin tins, or bake one batch and then the final 4 before freezing.

Meanwhile, cook the sausage in a large skillet, breaking it up as you cook. When sausage is cooked, add cream cheese, cooking on low heat until the cream cheese is melted. Stir well.

Bake the wonton wrappers at 350 for 8 minutes. When slightly brown, remove from oven and fill cups with the sausage mixture. Sprinkle with cheddar cheese. Bake another 5 minutes or until the cheese is melted. Cool, place into freezer bags and freeze.

When you're ready to eat: Heat these from frozen. Place the desired number of cups on a baking sheet and bake at 350 for about 15-20 minutes or until hot.

Part 2

Homemade Chicken Bowls

Ingredients
- 1 1/4 pounds yellow-fleshed potatoes, peeled and thinly sliced
- 2 cloves garlic, smashed
- 5 tablespoons extra-virgin olive oil
- 2 large skinless, boneless chicken breasts
- Salt and pepper
- 1 small onion, finely chopped
- 1/2 teaspoon dried thyme
- 2 cups chicken broth
- 1 cup frozen peas and carrots
- 1 cup small broccoli florets
- 2 tablespoons cornstarch
- 1 teaspoon Dijon mustard

Directions

In a medium saucepan, combine the potatoes, garlic and enough salted water to cover.

Bring to a boil, then simmer until the potatoes are tender, about 15 minutes; drain, reserving 1/4 cup of the cooking water.

Meanwhile, in a medium skillet, heat 2 tablespoons olive oil over medium-high heat.

Add the chicken and cook for 4 minutes on each side.

Transfer to a plate and shred; season with salt.

In the same skillet, add the onion and thyme and cook, stirring, over medium-high heat for 2 minutes.

Add 1 1/2 cups chicken broth and bring to a boil, scraping up any browned bits.

Lower the heat to medium, add the peas and carrots and broccoli and cook for 2 minutes.

In a bowl, stir the cornstarch into the remaining 1/2 cup broth, then stir into the vegetable mixture.

Bring to a boil and cook until thickened.

Stir in the chicken and mustard; season with salt and pepper. Keep warm.

In a bowl, mash the potatoes with the remaining 3 tablespoons olive oil and the reserved cooking water.

Divide among 4 shallow bowls, make a well in the center and top with the chicken and vegetables.

Freeze:

Cool prepared meal completely. Cover with foil; freeze up to 2 months.

Spinach & Noodle Casserole

Ingredients
- 2 12 ounce packages frozen chopped organic spinach
- Salt and pepper
- 1 pound extra-wide egg noodles
- 1 tablespoon extra-virgin olive oil
- 1 medium onion, finely chopped
- 2 cloves garlic, finely chopped
- 3 tablespoons butter
- 2 rounded tablespoons flour
- 2 cups whole milk
- Freshly grated nutmeg
- 2 egg yolks
- 1 cup panko or whole wheat panko breadcrumbs
- 1 cup shredded gruyere cheese
- 1/2 cup shredded parmigiano reggiano

Directions

In a microwave, defrost the spinach, then wring dry in a clean kitchen towel.

Bring a large pot of water to a boil, salt it, add the pasta and cook until al dente. Drain and return the noodles to the pot.

While the pasta is working, in a medium skillet, heat the oven, 1 turn of the pan, over medium heat.

Add the onion and garlic and cook until tender, 8 to 10 minutes.

Add the spinach, breaking it apart, to heat through.

Season with salt and pepper. Remove the pan from the heat.

Position an oven rack in the center of the oven and preheat the broiler.

While the onion cooks, in a medium saucepan, melt the butter over medium heat.

Whisk in the flour for 1 minute, then whisk in the milk; season with salt, pepper and nutmeg.

Cook until thickened, about 5 minutes. In a bowl, whisk a little of the sauce into the egg yolks, then whisk the egg yolk mixture into the sauce in the pan and turn the heat to the lowest setting.

In a bowl, mix together the panko, gruyere and parmigiano-reggiano.

Stir the spinach and sauce into the noodles to combine, then transfer to a casserole dish.

Top with the panko-cheese mixture.

Broil in the middle of the oven until bubbly and brown, 3 to 5 minutes.

Freeze:

Cool prepared meal completely. Cover with foil; freeze up to 2 months.

Sirloin & Okra Stew

Ingredients

- 1 1/2 cups rice
- 3 tablespoons extra-virgin olive oil
- 1 1/2 pounds beef sirloin, cut into 3/4-inch cubes
- Salt and pepper
- 1 onion, chopped
- 1 28 ounce can diced fire-roasted tomatoes
- 1 16 ounce bag frozen cut okra
- 1 cup beef broth
- 1/2 cup chopped parsley

Directions

In a medium saucepan, combine the rice and 3 cups water.

Bring to a simmer, cover and cook over medium-low heat until the water is absorbed, about 20 minutes.

Remove from the heat and let stand, covered, for 5 minutes before fluffing with a fork.

While the rice is cooking, in a large pot, heat 2 tablespoons olive oil over medium-high heat.

Season the beef with salt and pepper.

Working in batches, add the beef and cook until browned, about 2 minutes; transfer to a bowl.

Lower the heat to medium, add the onion and remaining 1 tablespoon olive oil to the pot and cook until translucent, 3 to 4 minutes.

Stir in the tomatoes, okra and beef broth; bring to a boil, stirring occasionally, then lower the heat and simmer until thickened, about 15 minutes.

Return the beef and any juices to the pot and stir in the parsley.

Serve with the rice.

Freeze:

Cool prepared meal completely. Cover with foil; freeze up to 2 months.

Pepperoni Pizza Puffs

Ingredients

- 3/4 cup flour
- 3/4 teaspoon baking powder
- 3/4 cup whole milk
- 1 egg, lightly beaten
- 4 ounces cheese, shredded
- 4 ounces pepperoni, cut into small cubes
- 1/2 cup store-bought pizza sauce
- 2 tablespoons finely chopped fresh basil
- 1 red bell pepper, sliced

Directions

Preheat the oven to 375 degrees . Grease a 24-cup mini-muffin pan.

In a large bowl, whisk together the flour and baking powder; whisk in the milk and egg.

Stir in the mozzarella and pepperoni; let stand for 10 minutes.

Stir the batter and divide among the mini-muffin cups.

Bake until puffed and golden, 20 to 25 minutes.

Meanwhile, microwave the pizza sauce until warmed through, then stir in 1 tablespoon basil.

Sprinkle the puffs with the remaining 1 tablespoon basil.

Serve the puffs and red pepper slices with the pizza sauce for dipping.

Freeze:

Cool prepared meal completely. Cover with foil; freeze up to 2 months.

Easy Casserole

Ingredients
- 1/2 pound sliced baked ham, torn into small pieces
- 7 ounces cornbread, cut into small cubes
- 1 cup frozen peas, thawed
- 1 teaspoon chopped fresh thyme
- 2 cups whole milk
- 3 eggs plus one yolk, lightly beaten
- Salt

Directions

Preheat the oven to 350 degrees . Lightly butter a 9-inch casserole dish.

In a bowl, toss the ham, cornbread, peas and thyme; transfer to the baking dish.

In the same bowl, beat together the milk, eggs and yolk and salt.

Pour into the baking dish. Let stand for 15 minutes.

Bake until the custard is just set in the center, 40 to 45 minutes.

Let stand for 10 minutes before serving. Serve with a green salad.

Freeze:

Cool prepared meal completely. Cover with foil; freeze up to 2 months.

Shrimp Spaghetti

Ingredients
- 2 13 1/2 ounce can coconut milk
- 1 14 1/2 ounce can chicken broth
- 1 tablespoon Asian fish sauce
- 1 tablespoon finely chopped garlic
- 2 teaspoons finely chopped ginger
- 2 teaspoons hot chili sauce
- 2 x 2 pound bag frozen, raw shrimp, thawed and tails removed
- 1 bunch cilantro, coarsely chopped
- 1 1/2 pounds spaghetti

Directions

In a large, deep skillet, bring the coconut milk and chicken broth to a simmer over medium heat.

Stir in the fish sauce, garlic, ginger, chili sauce and lime juice and cook for 2 minutes.

Stir in the shrimp and cook until just opaque, about 4 minutes.

Stir in the cilantro and remove from the heat.

Transfer two-thirds of the shrimp mixture to a bowl; let cool.

In a large pot of boiling, salted water, cook the spaghetti until al dente; drain.

Using tongs, transfer one-third of the pasta to the skillet of shrimp.

Cook one meal now: Toss the pasta with the shrimp mixture and simmer until warmed through, 1 to 2 minutes.

Freeze two meals for later: Divide the remaining shrimp mixture between 2 resealable 1-gallon freezer bags; seal.

Divide the remaining spaghetti between 2 more freezer bags; let cool, then seal. Label each and freeze.

THAW 1 bag each of the shrimp mixture and pasta per meal in the refrigerator overnight.

Freeze:

Cool prepared meal completely. Cover with foil; freeze up to 2 months.

Beef Kebabs

Ingredients

- 1 pound ground beef
- 1/4 cup chopped flat-leaf parsley
- 1 tablespoon finely chopped garlic
- 1 teaspoon smoked paprika
- Salt and pepper
- 1 1/4 pounds green beans
- 1 1/2 tablespoons extra-virgin olive oil
- 2 tablespoons sliced almonds
- 1/2 lemon, cut into 4 wedges

Directions
Preheat the oven to 450 degrees.

In a large bowl, crumble the beef and mix in the parsley, garlic, paprika, 1 teaspoon salt and 1/2 teaspoon pepper.

Form into sixteen 1 1/4-inch balls and thread onto 4 skewers.

On a rimmed baking sheet, toss the green beans with the olive oil and 1/4 teaspoon each salt and pepper; spread out in a single layer.

Roast for 10 minutes, then stir in the almonds and roast until the green beans are lightly browned and the almonds are toasted, about 5 minutes.

Meanwhile, preheat a grill pan to medium-high.

Grill the meatballs, turning, until just cooked through, 8 to 10 minutes.

Serve with the green beans and lemon wedges.

Freeze:

Cool prepared meal completely. Cover with foil; freeze up to 2 months.

Sweet Pea & Chicken Pasta

Ingredients

- 1 lemon, 1/2 thinly sliced crosswise, 1/2 squeezed into juice
- 4 chicken leg quarters
- 1 tablespoon vegetable oil
- Salt and pepper
- 1/2 ounce peas, thawed
- 1/4 cup ricotta cheese
- 1 tablespoon chopped fresh tarragon
- 24 wonton wrappers

Directions

Preheat the oven to 425 degrees.

Arrange the lemon slices in a single layer down the center of a roasting pan.

Rub the chicken with the oil and season with salt and pepper.

Place the chicken skin side up on the lemon slices and bake for 35 minutes.

Transfer to the broiler and cook until the skin is crisp, about 3 minutes.

Drizzle the chicken with the lemon juice.

Meanwhile, using a food processor, mix together the peas, ricotta, 1/2 teaspoon tarragon and 1/4 teaspoon salt.

On a work surface, working with 2 wonton wrappers at a time, spoon a teaspoon of the pea mixture onto the center of each wrapper.

Moisten the edges with water and fold the wrapper in half diagonally to form a triangle, pushing out any air pockets and pressing the edges firmly to seal.

With the long side of the triangle facing you, fold the top point back toward you, then fold the right and left points to meet it and press all 3 points firmly together, securing with more water.

In a large pot of boiling, salted water, cook the tortellini until they float to the top, about 5 minutes.

Using a slotted spoon, transfer the tortellini to 4 plates.

Divide the chicken and roasted lemon slices among the plates and top with the pan juices.

Sprinkle with the remaining 2 1/2 teaspoons tarragon.

Freeze:

Cool prepared meal completely. Cover with foil; freeze up to 2 months.

Jacks Sausage & Shrimp

Ingredients

- 2 2 pound bags frozen, raw shrimp
- 1/4 cup extra-virgin olive oil
- 2 tablespoons butter
- 4 cups long-grain white rice
- 1 large onion, chopped
- 4 links precooked chicken-apple sausage, cut into 1-inch pieces
- 1 large green bell pepper, chopped
- 2 teaspoons finely chopped garlic
- 1 14 1/2 ounce can diced tomatoes
- Salt and pepper
- 6 cups chicken broth

Directions

Divide the shrimp into 3 portions: Place 1 portion in a large bowl of cold water to thaw.

Place 1 each of the remaining portions in 2 resealable 1-gallon freezer bags; label and freeze.

Meanwhile, in a large, deep skillet, heat the olive oil and butter over medium-high heat.

Add the rice and onion and cook, stirring occasionally, until the onion is softened, about 5 minutes.

Add the sausage, bell pepper and garlic and cook, stirring, until the vegetables are softened, about 3 minutes.

Remove from the heat and stir in the tomatoes and their juices; season with salt and pepper.

Transfer two-thirds of the rice mixture to a bowl; let cool.

Stir 2 cups chicken broth into the rice in the skillet.

Cook one meal now: Bring the rice mixture to a boil, lower the heat, cover and simmer until the rice is tender, about 17 minutes.

Drain the thawed shrimp and add to the rice mixture.

Cook over medium heat, stirring often, until opaque, about 5 minutes.

Pour 2 cups chicken broth into each freezer bag; seal, label and freeze.

Freeze:

Cool prepared meal completely. Cover with foil; freeze up to 2 months.

Chicken Drumsticks

Ingredients
- 3 pounds chicken drumsticks , rinsed and patted dry
- 7 tablespoons butter
- Salt and pepper
- 3 cloves unpeeled garlic
- 1 large sweet potato
- 1/2 cup finely chopped onion
- 3/4 cup flour
- 1/3 cup chicken broth
- 2 large eggs
- 1 cup breadcrumbs, preferably panko
- 1/2 cup vegetable oil
- Lemon wedges, for serving

Directions

Preheat the oven to 425 degrees.

Place the chicken on a foil-lined rimmed baking sheet, rub all over with 2 tablespoons butter and season with salt and pepper.

Wrap the garlic cloves in foil and set on the baking sheet.

Roast until the chicken juices run clear, about 45 minutes.

Set the roasted garlic aside and let the chicken cool for 15 minutes.

Discard the skin and bones and finely chop the meat; set aside.

Meanwhile, pierce the sweet potato in several places and place on a paper towel in the microwave oven.

Cook on high for 6 minutes. Turn over and cook until tender, 6 to 10 minutes more.

Cover with a paper towel and let stand for 5 minutes.

Peel the potato and the reserved roasted garlic and transfer to a large bowl; mash and set aside.

In a small saucepan, melt the remaining 5 tablespoons butter over low heat.

Add the onion and cook until softened, about 10 minutes.

Stir in 1/4 cup flour and cook over low heat, stirring constantly, for 3 minutes.

Slowly add the chicken broth, stirring until a paste forms, then cook for 3 minutes, stirring occasionally.

Stir the paste into the reserved mashed potato mixture.

Stir in the reserved chicken. Season with salt and pepper.

Cover with plastic wrap and refrigerate until firm, about 30 minutes.

Meanwhile, in a small bowl, beat the eggs with 1 tablespoon water.

Place the remaining 1/2 cup flour and the breadcrumbs on separate plates.

Divide the croquette mixture into eight 1/2-inch-thick oval disks.

Coat with the flour and shake off any excess.

Dip in the egg mixture, letting the excess drip off, then coat with the bread crumbs.

Place the breaded croquettes on wax paper.

In a small skillet, heat the oil over high heat until hot but not smoking.

Working in 2 batches, fry the croquettes until golden brown, 1 to 1-1/2 minutes per side.

Using a slotted spoon, transfer to paper towels to drain.

Serve 2 croquettes, with a lemon wedge, per person.

Freeze:

Cool prepared meal completely. Cover with foil; freeze up to 2 months.

Dumplings With Chicken

Ingredients
- 3 pounds chicken drumsticks, rinsed and patted dry
- Salt and pepper
- 2/3 pound baking potatoes, peeled
- 2 tablespoons butter
- 2 cups finely chopped yellow onion
- 6 cups chicken broth
- 1 large egg
- 1/2 cup plus 2 tablespoons flour, plus more for kneading
- Chopped fresh parsley, for garnish

Directions
Preheat the oven to 425 degrees.

Place the chicken on a rimmed baking sheet and season with salt and pepper.

Roast until the juices run clear, about 45 minutes.

Let cool and then shred; discard the skin and bones.

Meanwhile, place the potatoes in a medium saucepan with enough cold water to cover by 1 inch.

Bring to a boil, then simmer until, about 45 minutes. Drain.

In a large pot, melt the butter over medium heat.

Add the onion and cook, stirring often, until softened, about 8 minutes.

Pour in the broth and bring to a gentle simmer.

Meanwhile, mash the potatoes with 1 teaspoon salt until almost smooth.

Mix in the egg, then the flour, until combined.

On a lightly floured surface, roll one-third of the dough into a 3/4-inch thick log.

Pinch off inch-long pieces and roll to form small disks.

Repeat with the remaining dough.

Add the dumplings to the broth.

Once they float, cook for 3 to 4 minutes more.

Stir in the reserved chicken and season with salt and pepper.

Top with the parsley.

Freeze:

Cool prepared meal completely. Cover with foil; freeze up to 2 months.

Seafood Tortillas

Ingredients
- 2 tablespoons butter

- 2x 2 pound bags frozen raw shrimp, thawed and tails removed

- 1 tablespoon finely chopped garlic

- Salt and pepper

- 1 lemon, halved

- 3 chipotle chiles in adobo sauce, plus 1 tablespoon adobo sauce

- 12 10-inch flour tortillas

- 1 pound gouda cheese, shredded

Directions
In a large, deep skillet, melt the butter over medium-high heat.

Add the shrimp, garlic, 1/2 teaspoon salt and 1/2 teaspoon pepper.

Increase the heat to high and cook, stirring often, until the shrimp are just opaque, about 4 minutes.

Squeeze the lemon halves over the shrimp.

In a small bowl, mash the chipotles with the adobo sauce.

Spread the paste in a thin layer on each tortilla.

Cover half of each tortilla with a single layer of shrimp.

Sprinkle the cheese over the shrimp; fold the tortillas in half.

Cook one meal now: In a large nonstick skillet, working in 2 batches, cook 2 quesadillas, cheese side down, over medium-high heat until golden, about 2 minutes on each side. Cut into wedges.

Freeze: Wrap each quesadilla in foil and stack 4 each into 2 resealable 1-gallon freezer bags; seal, label and freeze.

European Meatball Stew

Ingredients
- 1 1/2 pounds ground beef

- 1/2 cup bread crumbs

- 1 large egg

- Salt and pepper

- 2 tablespoons extra-virgin olive oil

- 2 carrots, chopped

- 1 small onion, chopped

- 1 rib celery, chopped

- 2 tablespoons flour

- 2 tablespoons sweet paprika

- 2 cups beef broth

- 1 tablespoon caraway seeds

Directions
In a large bowl, combine the beef, breadcrumbs, egg, 1 teaspoon salt and 1/4 teaspoon pepper.

Mix well and form into 1 1/2-inch meatballs.

In a large skillet, heat the olive oil over medium-high heat.

Working in 2 batches, add the meatballs and cook, shaking the skillet often, until lightly browned, 5 to 7 minutes.

Transfer to paper towels to drain.

Pour off all but 1 tablespoon of the fat in the skillet and add the carrots, onion and celery.

Cook, stirring constantly, until softened, about 3 minutes.

Stir in the flour and paprika and cook for 1 minute.

Pour in the beef broth and bring to a boil over high heat, scraping up any browned bits from the bottom of the pan; season to taste with salt and pepper.

Add the reserved meatballs and caraway seeds, reduce the heat to medium-low and simmer for 5 minutes.

Serve with buttered noodles.

Freeze:

Cool prepared meal completely. Cover with foil; freeze up to 2 months.

Beef Pot

Ingredients
- 6 tablespoons butter, chilled
- 1 small onion, chopped
- 1 1/2 pounds ground beef
- 1 28 ounce can diced tomatoes, drained
- 1 cup beef broth
- Salt and pepper
- 1 1/2 cups flour
- 2 teaspoons baking powder
- 2 cups shredded sharp cheddar cheese
- 1/2 cup milk

Directions

Preheat the oven to 375 degrees.

Grease an 8-by-12-inch baking dish and set aside.

In a large skillet, heat 2 tablespoons butter over medium-high heat.

Add the onion and cook, stirring, until softened but not browned, 3 to 5 minutes.

Add the beef and cook, breaking it up with the back of a spoon, until no longer pink, about 5 minutes.

Stir in the tomatoes and beef broth and season with salt and pepper.

Lower the heat and cook, stirring occasionally, until most of the liquid has cooked off, about 20 minutes.

Pour into the prepared baking dish and spread evenly.

Meanwhile, in a large bowl, combine the flour, baking powder and 1/2 teaspoon salt.

Using your fingertips or a pastry blender, blend in the remaining 4 tablespoons butter and the cheese until the mixture resembles coarse crumbs.

Pour in the milk and stir quickly with a fork to form a dry, shaggy dough.

Gather the dough together and knead lightly in the bowl.

Transfer to a floured work surface and roll or pat into a large, 1/2-inch-thick round.

Using a 3-inch cookie cutter, cut out 8 biscuits.

Gather the scraps of dough, form into a new round and cut out more biscuits.

Continue until all the dough has been used.

Place the biscuits on top of the beef mixture as close together as possible and bake until lightly browned, about 35 minutes.

Freeze:

Cool prepared meal completely. Cover with foil; freeze up to 2 months.

Grans Sausage Pie

Ingredients
- 1 1/2 teaspoons extra-virgin olive oil
- 1/2 pound bulk pork breakfast sausage
- 1/2 tablespoon chopped fresh oregano
- 4 pieces refrigerated biscuit dough
- 1 red onion, thinly sliced
- 2 ounces crumbled feta cheese
- 1/4 cup kalamata olives, sliced
- 2 large eggs, plus 2 large egg yolks
- 1/2 cup milk
- Salt and pepper

Directions
Preheat the oven to 375 degrees.

In a large skillet, heat 1 teaspoon olive oil over medium-high heat.

Add the sausage and oregano and cook, breaking up the sausage, until just browned, about 5 minutes. Drain and let cool.

Grease a 9-inch pie pan with the remaining 1/2 teaspoon olive oil.

Place 1 piece biscuit dough into a large resealable plastic bag and, using a rolling pin, roll into a 1/8-inch-thick disk.

Remove the dough from the bag and transfer to the prepared pie pan.

Repeat with the remaining dough pieces, pinching the pieces together in the pan to form a crust.

In a large bowl, combine the cooked sausage, onion, feta and olives; spread evenly over the crust.

In a medium bowl, beat the eggs, egg yolks, milk and 1/8 teaspoon each salt and pepper.

Pour the egg mixture over the sausage mixture and bake until set, about 25 minutes.

Freeze:

Cool prepared meal completely. Cover with foil; freeze up to 2 months.

Chicken Tandoori & Couscous

Ingredients
- 1 cup whole milk yogurt
- Juice of 1/2 lemon
- 1 tablespoon finely chopped fresh ginger
- 1 clove garlic, minced
- 2 teaspoons garam masala
- 3 pounds chicken drumsticks , rinsed and patted dry
- Salt
- 1 cup couscous
- 1/3 cup chopped pitted dates
- 1/2 cup sliced almonds, toasted
- 1/4 cup chopped fresh parsley

Directions
In a medium bowl, stir together the yogurt, lemon juice, ginger, garlic and garam masala.

Transfer the yogurt mixture to a large resealable plastic bag and add the chicken, being sure to coat each piece.

Refrigerate for at least 1 hour or overnight.

Preheat the oven to 425 degrees.

Place the chicken on a foil-lined rimmed baking sheet, season with salt and roast until juices run clear, about 45 minutes.

Let the chicken stand for 5 minutes before serving.

Meanwhile, in a medium saucepan, bring 1-1/2 cups salted water to a boil.

Remove from the heat and stir in the couscous and dates.

Cover and let stand for 5 minutes. Uncover and fluff with a fork.

Stir in the toasted almonds and parsley. Serve with the chicken.

Freeze:

Cool prepared meal completely. Cover with foil; freeze up to 2 months.

Beef Meatloaf

Ingredients
- 2 tablespoons extra-virgin olive oil

- 1 red onion, finely chopped

- 2/3 cup ketchup

- 2/3 cup bread crumbs

- 2 large eggs

- 1/2 cup bread-and-butter pickle chips, chopped

- 1 1/2 pounds ground beef

- 8 ounces cheddar cheese, cut into 1/3-inch cubes

- 2 pounds new red potatoes

- 3/4 cup heavy cream

Directions

Preheat the oven to 400 degrees . Lightly oil a rimmed baking sheet.

In a medium skillet, heat 2 tablespoons olive oil over medium heat.

Add the onion and cook, stirring until slightly softened, about 3 minutes.

In a large bowl, combine the ketchup, bread crumbs, eggs and pickles; mix in the onion.

Crumble in the beef, add the cheese and mix together.

Transfer to the prepared baking sheet and shape into a 4-by-12-inch loaf.

Bake until an instant-read thermometer inserted into the center registers 160 degrees, about 35 minutes.

Meanwhile, halve the potatoes and place them in a large pot with enough salted water to cover by an inch.

Bring to a boil, then lower the heat and simmer until tender, 10 to 15 minutes. Drain, return to the pot and mash with the cream.

Let the meatloaf rest for 5 minutes before slicing. Serve with the mashed potatoes.

Freeze:

Cool prepared meal completely. Cover with foil; freeze up to 2 months.

Chicken Casserole

Ingredients

- 1 medium to large rotisserie chicken
- 7 tablespoons unsalted butter, plus more for greasing the dish
- 8 ounces white mushrooms, thinly sliced
- 1 medium onion, finely chopped
- 2 celery ribs, finely chopped
- 2 tablespoons all-purpose flour
- 1 cup chicken broth
- 1 cup milk
- 1 teaspoon fresh lemon juice
- Salt and freshly ground pepper
- 3 garlic cloves, finely chopped
- 2 cups baking mix, such as Bisquick
- 1/2 cup shredded cheddar cheese

Directions

Preheat the oven to 425 degrees . Butter a large casserole dish.

Pull the meat off the chicken, shredding it with your fingers or a fork into the baking dish.

In a large skillet, melt 3 tablespoons of the butter over high heat.

Add the mushrooms, onion and celery and cook, stirring occasionally, until the mushrooms are browned, about 6 minutes.

Lower the heat to medium, sprinkle the flour into the skillet and cook, stirring, for 1 minute.

Stir in the chicken broth, bring to a simmer and cook, stirring, until thickened, about 2 minutes.

Stir in 1/3 cup of the milk and simmer for 1 minute more.

Remove the skillet from the heat, add the lemon juice, and add salt and pepper to taste.

Pour the gravy over the chicken in the baking dish.

Melt the remaining 4 tablespoons of butter with the garlic.

Stir together the baking mix, the remaining 2/3 cup of milk and the cheese.

Drop tablespoonfuls of the biscuit mixture on top of the casserole and brush with half of the garlic butter.

Bake until the biscuits are golden brown, about 25 minutes, brushing them once or twice with the remaining garlic butter.

Freeze:

Cool prepared meal completely. Cover with foil; freeze up to 2 months.

Mexican Turkey Casserole

Ingredients
- 2 limes, quartered

- 1 pound turkey breast cutlets

- Salt

- 1 large onion, finely chopped

- 1 4 ounce can diced jalapeno chiles, liquid reserved

- 2 14 1/2 ounce can fire-roasted diced tomatoes

- 1 1 bag tortilla chips, lightly crushed

- 1 14 1/2 ounce cans chicken broth

- 1 pound Mexican shredded cheese blend 1 cup sour cream

Directions
Preheat a grill pan to medium-high.

Squeeze the limes over the turkey cutlets; season with salt.

Grill the turkey until just cooked through, 3 to 4 minutes per side. Let cool, then slice into 2-inch-long strips.

Preheat the oven to 375 degrees.

In a large bowl, combine the onion, the jalapenos with their liquid and the tomatoes.

Add the tortilla chips and turkey and toss well. Transfer the mixture to a greased 9-by-12-inch baking dish.

Drizzle with the chicken broth and top with the cheese. Bake until the cheese is golden around the edges, about 40 minutes. Serve with the sour cream.

Freeze:

Cool prepared meal completely. Cover with foil; freeze up to 2 months.

Beef Moussaka

Ingredients
- 4 tablespoons butter

- 1 small onion, chopped

- 1 1/2 pounds ground beef

- 2 teaspoons ground cinnamon

- 1 teaspoon ground nutmeg

- Salt and pepper

- 1 8 ounce can tomato sauce

- 2 large eggs

- 2 tablespoons flour

- 1 cup whole milk

- 4 ounces cream cheese

- 1/2 cup ricotta cheese

Directions
Preheat the oven to 350 degrees.

In a large skillet, heat 2 tablespoons butter over medium-high heat.

Add the onion and cook until softened, 3 to 5 minutes.

Add the beef and cook until no longer pink, about 5 minutes.

Stir in the cinnamon and nutmeg and season with salt and pepper.

Add the tomato sauce and cook until most of the liquid has evaporated, 3 to 5 minutes.

Pour into an 8-inch square baking dish and set aside.

In a medium bowl, lightly beat the eggs and set aside. In a small saucepan, melt the remaining 2 tablespoons butter over medium-high heat.

Whisk in the flour and cook, whisking often, until the mixture is smooth, about 30 seconds.

Slowly whisk in the milk until thickened.

Lower the heat to medium and stir in the cream cheese and ricotta; season with salt and pepper.

Whisk one-quarter of the cheese sauce into the reserved eggs until smooth.

Whisk the egg mixture into the cheese sauce in the saucepan.

Pour the sauce over the meat in the baking dish and spread evenly.

Bake until the top is lightly browned and firm to the touch, 40 to 45 minutes.

Let cool for 10 minutes; cut into squares to serve.

Freeze:

Cool prepared meal completely. Cover with foil; freeze up to 2 months.

Greek Lamb Meatballs

Ingredients
- 2 tbsp olive oil
- 2 red onions, very finely chopped
- 4 garlic cloves, crushed
- 2 tsp each ground cumin and coriander
- 400g can chopped tomatoes
- ½ tsp sugar
- ½ 20g pack mint finely chopped
- 500g pack lean lamb mince
- 8 dried apricot, finely chopped
- 50g fresh breadcrumbs
- pitta bread and salad, to serve

Method

Heat 2 tsp oil in a pan and soften the onions for 5 mins.

Add the garlic and spices and cook for a few mins more.

Spoon half the onion mixture into a bowl and set aside to cool.

Add the tomatoes, sugar and seasoning to the remaining onions in the pan and simmer for about 10 mins until reduced.

Meanwhile, add the mint, lamb, apricots and breadcrumbs to the cooled onions, season and mix well with your hands.

Shape into little meatballs.

Heat the rest of the oil in a non-stick pan and fry the meatballs until golden.

Stir in the sauce with a splash of water and gently cook everything for a few mins until the meatballs are cooked through.

Serve with pitta bread and salad.

Freeze:

Cool prepared meal completely. Cover with foil; freeze up to 2 months.

Great Lamb Dish

Ingredients
- 2 tbsp olive oil
- 1 onion, finely diced
- 2 carrot, finely diced
- 500g diced leg of lamb
- 2 fat cloves garlic, crushed
- ½ tsp cumin
- ½ tsp ground ginger
- ¼ tsp saffron
- 1 tsp ground cinnamon
- 1 tbsp clear honey
- 100g soft dried apricot, quartered
- 1 low-salt vegetable stock cube
- 1 small butternut squash, peeled, seeds removed, cut into 1cm dice
- steamed couscous
- chopped parsley

Method

Heat the olive oil in a heavy-based pan and add the onion and carrot.

Cook for 3- 4 mins until softened.

Add the diced lamb and brown all over.

Stir in the garlic and all the spices and cook for a few mins more or until the aromas are released.

Add the honey and apricots, crumble in the stock cube and pour over roughly 500ml boiling water or enough to cover the meat.

Give it a good stir and bring to the boil.

Turn down to a simmer, put the lid on and cook for 1 hour.

Remove the lid and cook for a further 30 mins, then stir in the squash.

Cook for 20 – 30 mins more until the squash is soft and the lamb is tender.

Serve alongside rice or couscous and sprinkle with parsley and pine nuts, if using.

Freeze:

Cool prepared meal completely. Cover with foil; freeze up to 2 months.

Hot Pilafs

Ingredients
- 1 tbsp vegetable oil
- 1 onion, finely chopped
- 2 garlic cloves, crushed
- 1cm piece ginger, finely chopped
- 1 tsp tomato purée
- 1 tsp ground cumin
- 1 tsp garam masala
- 200g basmati rice
- 850ml vegetable stock
- 140g red lentils, washed and drained
- 200g bag spinach
- leaves, chopped
- handful mint
- leaves, chopped
- 8 peppers

Method
Heat the oil in a large saucepan with a lid.

Add the onion, garlic and ginger, then gently cook for 5 mins until softened.

Stir in the tomato purée and spices, and cook for 1 min more.

Add the rice, stir to coat, then pour in the stock.

Bring to the boil, tip in the lentils, cover with the lid and leave to cook over a low heat for 15 mins, until the lentils and rice are cooked.

Stir through the spinach and mint.

Use a sharp knife to slice the top off each pepper.

Cut out the middle stalk and scoop out any seeds.

Carefully trim the bottoms slightly so they stand upright, but the filling won't fall out.

Fill each pepper with the rice mix and place the lid on top.

Bake or wrap tightly in cling film or freezer bags and freeze.

To cook, defrost peppers completely if frozen.

Heat oven to 200C/180C fan/gas 6.

Place the peppers on a lightly greased baking tray and cook for 25-30 mins or until the peppers have softened.

Serve with a green salad tossed with cucumber, herbs and a dollop of yogurt.

Freeze:

Cool prepared meal completely. Cover with foil; freeze up to 2 months.

Mixed Bolognese

Ingredients
- 2 tablespoons olive oil, divided

- 6 ounces 90% lean ground sirloin

- 6 ounces lean ground pork
- 2 cups chopped onion
- 1 tablespoon minced garlic
- 1 cup finely chopped carrot
- 1 cup finely chopped celery
- 2 (28-ounce) cans unsalted diced tomatoes, divided
- 1/3 cup dry red wine
- 1 tablespoon dried oregano
- 1 teaspoon kosher salt
- 1/2 teaspoon freshly ground black pepper
- 1 bay leaf
- 1/3 cup chopped fresh flat-leaf parsley
- 1/4 cup finely chopped fresh basil, divided
- 1 pound uncooked whole-grain ziti pasta
- 2 ounces Parmesan cheese, shaved

Method

Heat a large Dutch oven over medium heat.

Add 1 tablespoon oil to pan; swirl to coat.

Add beef and pork; cook 6 minutes or until browned, stirring to crumble.

Remove beef mixture from pan. Reduce heat to medium-low.

Add remaining 1 tablespoon oil to pan; swirl to coat.

Add onion and garlic; sauté 2 minutes.

Add carrot and celery; cook 5 minutes.

Add 1 can tomatoes, wine, oregano, salt, pepper, and bay leaf; bring to a boil.

Drain remaining 1 can tomatoes; add to pan.

Cover, reduce heat, and simmer 40 minutes, stirring occasionally.

Return beef and pork to pan; simmer 10 minutes.

Remove bay leaf, and discard.

Stir in chopped parsley and 2 tablespoons basil, or follow freezing instructions.

Cook pasta according to package Directions, omitting salt and fat; drain.

Add pasta to sauce; toss to coat.

Divide pasta among 8 bowls; top evenly with remaining 2 tablespoons basil and Parmesan cheese.

Freeze:

Cool prepared meal completely. Cover with foil; freeze up to 2 months.

Turkey Sausage Gumbo

Ingredients
- 2 center-cut bacon slices, chopped
- 3/4 cup chopped onion
- 1/2 cup chopped green bell pepper

- 1/2 cup chopped celery
- 2 large garlic cloves, minced
- 4 cups unsalted chicken stock
- 1/2 cup chopped yellow bell pepper
- 3/4 teaspoon kosher salt
- 6 ounces andouille sausage links, thinly sliced
- 1 (14.5-ounce) can unsalted diced tomatoes, undrained
- 1 (10-ounce) package sliced frozen okra
- 1/4 cup chopped fresh flat-leaf parsley
- 2 teaspoons chopped fresh thyme
- 9 ounces cooked skinless, boneless turkey breast, shredded
- 2 teaspoons filé powder
- 4 cups hot cooked rice

Method

Cook bacon in a large Dutch oven over medium heat 4 minutes or until crisp.

Remove bacon from pan with a slotted spoon.

Add onion, green bell pepper, celery, and garlic to drippings in pan; sauté 5 minutes.

Add stock, yellow bell pepper, salt, sausage, tomatoes, and okra to pan; bring to a boil.

Reduce heat, and simmer 20 minutes.

Stir in parsley, thyme, and turkey; cook 2 minutes or until thoroughly heated.

Remove pan from heat; stir in filé powder.

Divide rice among 8 bowls; top evenly with gumbo, or follow freezing instructions.

Sprinkle evenly with reserved bacon

Freeze:

Cool prepared meal completely. Cover with foil; freeze up to 2 months.

Chicken Lasagna

Ingredients
- 3 cups unsalted chicken stock
- 1 1/2 pounds skinless, boneless chicken thighs, trimmed
- 2 1/2 tablespoons olive oil
- 1 1/2 cups chopped onion
- 3 tablespoons minced garlic
- 1 1/2 teaspoons kosher salt, divided
- 1/2 teaspoon chopped fresh thyme
- 1/2 teaspoon crushed red pepper
- 10 ounce sliced cremini mushrooms
- 3 packages fresh spinach
- Cooking spray
- 1 1/2 cups 2% reduced-fat milk

- 1/2 cup all-purpose flour
- 1/4 teaspoon ground nutmeg
- 2 ounces Parmigiano-Reggiano cheese, grated
- 12 no-boil lasagna noodles
- 5 ounces part-skim mozzarella cheese, shredded

Method

Bring stock to a boil in a large saucepan over medium-high heat.

Add chicken; reduce heat, and simmer 18 to 20 minutes or until -chicken is done. Remove chicken from pan; reserve stock.

When cool enough to handle, shred with 2 forks.

2. Heat a large skillet over medium-high heat. Add oil; swirl to coat.

Add onion, garlic, 1/2 teaspoon salt, thyme, pepper, and mushrooms; sauté 8 minutes.

Stir in spinach, 1 package at a time, cooking 2 minutes after each addition or until spinach wilts before adding more.

Remove pan from heat; stir in chicken.

Preheat oven to 375°.

Coat 2 (8-inch) square baking dishes with cooking spray.

Combine milk, flour, and nutmeg, stirring with a whisk until smooth.

Bring reserved stock to a boil over medium-high heat.

Gradually add milk mixture to stock mixture, stirring constantly with a whisk.

Stir in remaining 1 teaspoon salt.

Cook 5 minutes or until thickened, stirring occasionally.

Remove pan from heat; stir in Parmigiano-Reggiano.

Pour 1/2 cup sauce into bottom of each baking dish.

Top each with 2 noodles, 1 cup chicken mixture, 1 cup sauce, and 1/4 cup mozzarella, making sure noodles are covered with sauce.

Repeat layers once with noodles, chicken mixture, and sauce.

Top dishes evenly with remaining 4 noodles, remaining sauce, and remaining 3/4 cup mozzarella.

Cover dishes tightly with foil coated with cooking spray.

Bake at 375° for 25 minutes.

Uncover and bake at 375° for 10 to 15 minutes or until browned and bubbly, or follow freezing instructions.

Let stand 5 minutes before serving.

Freeze:

Cool prepared meal completely. Cover with foil; freeze up to 2 months.

Turkey Pasta

Method
- 12 ounces uncooked penne pasta
- 3 tablespoons plus 2 teaspoons canola oil, divided
- 1 pound turkey cutlets

- 2 cups chopped onion
- 1 cup chopped celery
- 1 tablespoon chopped fresh thyme
- 3 (8-ounce) packages presliced mushrooms
- 1/2 cup dry white wine
- 1 1/4 teaspoons kosher salt, divided
- 3 cups 2% reduced-fat milk
- 3 tablespoons all-purpose flour
- 3 ounces 1/3-less-fat cream cheese, softened
- 2 ounces Parmesan cheese, grated and divided
- 1 ounce fontina cheese, shredded
- 1 teaspoon black pepper
- 2 cups frozen green peas, thawed
- 2 tablespoons chopped fresh parsley
- 2 tablespoons chopped fresh tarragon
- Cooking spray panko
- 1/2 cup whole-wheat

Method

Preheat oven to 350°.

Cook pasta according to package Directions, omitting salt and fat. Drain.

Place pasta in a large bowl.

Heat a large skillet over medium-high heat.

Add 1 tablespoon oil to pan; swirl to coat. Add turkey; cook 2 minutes on each side or until done.

Remove turkey from pan; cut into bite-sized pieces. Add turkey to pasta.

4. Return pan to medium-high heat. Add 2 tablespoons oil; swirl to coat.

Add onion and celery; sauté 10 minutes.

Add thyme and mushrooms; cook 15 minutes or until liquid evaporates.

Add wine to pan; cook 4 minutes or until liquid evaporates, scraping pan to loosen browned bits. Stir in 1/4 teaspoon salt.

Add mushroom mixture to pasta mixture.

Place pan over medium heat.

Combine milk and flour in a bowl, stirring with a whisk until smooth.

Add milk mixture to pan; cook 3 minutes or until slightly thickened, stirring frequently.

Stir in cream cheese, 1 ounce Parmesan, and fontina; cook 5 minutes.

Stir in remaining 1 teaspoon salt and pepper.

Stir milk mixture, peas, parsley, and tarragon, if desired, into pasta mixture.

Divide pasta mixture between 2 square glass or ceramic baking dishes coated with cooking spray.

6. Combine remaining 2 teaspoons oil, remaining 1 ounce Parmesan, and panko in a bowl; sprinkle evenly over tops of dishes.

Bake at 350° for 20 minutes or until browned and bubbly, or follow freezing instructions.

Freeze:

Cool prepared meal completely. Cover with foil; freeze up to 2 months.

Pork & Mushrooms

Ingredient
- 2 tablespoons dark sesame oil
- 3/4 cup thinly sliced green onions, divided
- 1 tablespoon minced garlic
- 1 tablespoon grated peeled fresh ginger
- 4 ounces thinly sliced shiitake mushroom caps
- 5 tablespoons lower-sodium soy sauce, divided
- 1 tablespoon hoisin sauce
- 1/2 teaspoon freshly ground black pepper
- 14 ounces lean ground pork
- 40 gyoza skins or round wonton wrappers
- Cornstarch
- 1/4 cup hot water
- 2 tablespoons brown sugar

- 2 tablespoons rice wine vinegar

- 1 1/2 tablespoons sambal oelek

- Cooking spray

Method

Heat a large skillet over high heat. Add oil to pan; swirl to coat.

Add 1/2 cup onions, garlic, ginger, and mushrooms; stir-fry 3 minutes.

Remove from pan; cool slightly.

Combine mushroom mixture, 1 tablespoon soy sauce, hoisin sauce, pepper, and pork in a medium bowl.

Arrange 8 gyoza skins on a clean work surface; cover remaining skins with a damp towel to keep them from drying.

Spoon about 1 1/2 teaspoons pork mixture in the center of each skin.

Moisten edges of skin with water.

Fold in half; press edges together with fingertips to seal.

Place on a baking sheet sprinkled with cornstarch; cover to prevent drying.

Repeat procedure with remaining gyoza skins and pork mixture.

Combine 1/4 cup hot water and brown sugar in a small bowl, stirring until sugar dissolves.

Add remaining 1/4 cup green onions, remaining 1/4 cup soy sauce, vinegar, and sambal, stirring with a whisk until well combined.

Heat a large heavy skillet over high heat.

Generously coat pan with cooking spray.

Add 10 pot stickers to pan; cook 30 seconds or until browned on one side.

Turn pot stickers over; carefully add 1/3 cup water to pan. Cover tightly; steam 4 minutes.

Repeat procedure in batches with remaining pot stickers and more water, or follow freezing instructions.

After cooking, serve pot stickers immediately with dipping sauce.

Freeze:

Cool prepared meal completely. Cover with foil; freeze up to 2 months.

Original Chicken Tikka Masala

Ingredients
- 2 tablespoons olive oil, divided

- 3 pounds skinless, boneless chicken thighs, cut into 1 1/2-inch cubes

- 2 teaspoons kosher salt, divided

- 2 teaspoons ground cumin

- 2 teaspoons ground cinnamon

- 1 cup finely chopped onion

- 3 tablespoons minced fresh garlic

- 2 tablespoons minced peeled fresh ginger

- 2 serrano chiles, minced

- 2 teaspoons garam masala
- 3/4 teaspoon ground red pepper
- 1/2 cup unsalted chicken stock
- 1/2 cup half-and-half
- 2 (26.5-ounce) boxes chopped tomatoes, undrained
- 1/4 cup butter
- 6 cups hot cooked basmati rice
- 1/2 cup chopped fresh cilantro

Methods

Heat 1 tablespoon oil in a large Dutch oven over medium-high heat.

Sprinkle chicken with 1 teaspoon salt, cumin, and cinnamon.

Add half of chicken to pan; cook 5 minutes or until browned, stirring once.

Remove chicken from pan. Repeat procedure with remaining chicken; remove from pan.

Add remaining 1 tablespoon oil, onion, garlic, ginger, and serrano to pan; sauté 1 minute.

Reduce heat to low; cook 5 minutes or until softened, stirring frequently.

Add garam masala and red pepper; cook 1 minute, stirring constantly.

Add remaining 1 teaspoon salt, stock, half-and-half, and tomatoes, scraping pan to loosen browned bits.

Bring to a boil over high heat. Reduce heat to low; stir in chicken.

Simmer 6 minutes or until chicken is done.

Remove from heat; stir in butter until butter melts.

Serve over rice, or follow freezing instructions. Sprinkle with cilantro.

Freeze:

Cool prepared meal completely. Cover with foil; freeze up to 2 months.

Mama's Stuffed Peppers

Ingredients
- 8 large poblano peppers
- 4 dried ancho chiles
- 2 tablespoons canola oil
- 3 cups chopped onion
- 10 garlic cloves, minced
- 1 teaspoon kosher salt, divided
- 1 teaspoon black pepper
- 12 ounces 90% lean ground sirloin
- 4 ounces 1/3-less-fat cream cheese, softened
- 1 1/2 cups precooked brown rice
- 6 ounces queso fresco, crumbled and divided

- 1/4 cup fresh lime juice
- 1 tablespoon ground cumin
- 2 teaspoons sugar
- 2 cans unsalted diced tomatoes, undrained
- Cooking spray
- 1/4 cup cilantro leaves

Methods
Preheat broiler.

Place poblanos on a foil-lined baking sheet; broil 3 inches from heat 12 minutes or until blackened, turning after 6 minutes.

Place in a paper bag; fold to close tightly. Let stand 15 minutes.

Peel and discard skins. Cut a lengthwise slit in each pepper; discard seeds and membranes. Set aside.

While poblanos broil, place ancho chiles in a bowl. Cover with boiling water; let stand 10 minutes. Drain.

Reduce oven temperature to 400°.

Heat a large skillet over medium heat. Add oil to pan; swirl to coat.

Add onion and garlic; cook 4 minutes or until crisp-tender.

Reserve half of onion mixture. Add 1/2 teaspoon salt, black pepper, and beef; cook 8 minutes or until beef is done, stirring to crumble.

Remove from heat. Add cream cheese, stirring until well combined.

Stir in rice and half of queso fresco.

Place ancho chiles, reserved onion mixture, juice, cumin, sugar, tomatoes, and remaining 1/2 teaspoon salt in a blender; process until smooth.

Pour 1 cup sauce into each of 2 square glass or ceramic baking dishes coated with cooking spray.

Open each poblano chile; flatten slightly with hand.

Divide beef mixture evenly among chiles.

Arrange 4 chiles in each dish; top evenly with remaining sauce and queso.

Bake at 400° for 20 minutes or until bubbly, or follow freezing instructions.

Sprinkle with cilantro after cooking.

Freeze:

Cool prepared meal completely. Cover with foil; freeze up to 2 months.

Easy Chicken Pizzas

Ingredients
- 30 ounces refrigerated fresh pizza dough, divided

- 1/2 cup olive oil

- 1/4 cup chopped fresh basil

- 1 teaspoon crushed red pepper

- 8 garlic cloves, crushed

- 4 thyme sprigs

- 4 cups 2% reduced-fat milk

- 1 cup plain fat-free Greek yogurt

- 4 teaspoons cider vinegar

- 1/2 teaspoon kosher salt

- 12 ounces shredded cooked chicken breast

- 6.5 ounces pre shredded reduced-fat 4-cheese Italian-blend

- 3 ounces fresh part-skim mozzarella cheese, torn into small pieces

- 2 tablespoons fresh thyme leaves

- 1 1/2 teaspoons freshly ground black pepper

- 1/2 cup small fresh basil leave

Methods

Place a pizza stone or heavy baking sheet in oven. Preheat oven to 450°

Let pizza dough rest, covered, at room temperature as oven preheats.

Combine oil and next 4 Ingredients in a small saucepan over medium heat.

Cook 4 minutes or until garlic begins to brown, stirring frequently.

Remove from heat; let stand 5 minutes.

Strain mixture through a fine sieve over a small bowl; discard solids.

Combine milk, yogurt, and vinegar in a large microwave-safe bowl.

Microwave at HIGH 6 minutes. Gently stir to form small curds.

Strain curds through a fine sieve; let stand 5 minutes. Discard liquid.

Combine oil mixture, cheese curds, and salt, stirring gently.

Divide dough into 12 equal pieces.

Roll each piece into a 6-inch circle on a lightly floured surface.

Spread about 1 1/2 tablespoons oil mixture over each pizza, leaving a 1/2-inch border.

Divide chicken, Italian-blend cheese, and mozzarella cheese evenly among pizzas; sprinkle evenly with thyme leaves and black pepper.

Carefully remove pizza stone from oven.

Arrange 3 to 4 pizzas on pizza stone.

Bake at 450° for 8 minutes or until dough is golden and cheese browns.

Repeat procedure with remaining pizzas, or follow freezing instructions.

Sprinkle pizzas evenly with fresh basil leaves.

Freeze:

Cool prepared meal completely. Cover with foil; freeze up to 2 months.

Mexican Chili

Ingredients
- 12 ounces uncooked rotini, or spiral macaroni, pasta

- 2 cups canned red kidney beans, rinsed and drained

- 2 tablespoons olive oil

- 2 cups chopped onion
- 2 tablespoons minced fresh garlic
- 1 pound cremini mushrooms, finely chopped
- 20 ounces ground turkey breast
- 2 cups chopped green bell pepper
- 4 teaspoons ground cumin
- 2 teaspoons dried oregano
- 1 teaspoon kosher salt
- 1 teaspoon smoked paprika
- 1 teaspoon ancho chile powder
- 1 teaspoon freshly ground black pepper
- 1/4 to 1 teaspoon ground red pepper
- 4 cups lower-sodium marinara sauce
- Cooking spray
- 4 ounces extra-sharp cheddar cheese, shredded

Methods

Preheat oven to 350°.

Cook pasta in boiling water until almost al dente. Drain.

Combine pasta and beans in a large bowl.

Heat a large skillet over medium heat. Add oil to pan; swirl to coat.

Add onion, garlic, and mushrooms to pan; cook 11 minutes or until liquid almost evaporates.

Add turkey; cook 5 minutes or until done, stirring to crumble.

Add bell pepper and next 7 Ingredients; cook 1 minute.

Stir in marinara sauce; bring to a boil. Add marinara mixture to pasta mixture; toss to coat.

Divide mixture evenly between 2 glass baking dishes coated with cooking spray. Top evenly with cheese.

Bake at 350° for 10 minutes or until cheese melts, or follow freezing instructions.

Freeze:

Cool prepared meal completely. Cover with foil; freeze up to 2 months.

Asian Curry Stew

Ingredients
- 1 1/2 tablespoons butter
- 1 package pre chopped onion
- 2 garlic cloves, minced
- 3 tablespoons green curry paste
- 1 tablespoon minced peeled fresh ginger
- 1 teaspoon ground cumin
- 1 1/2 tablespoons lower-sodium soy sauce
- 2 cans light coconut milk
- 1 package trimmed green beans, cut into 1-inch pieces
- 2 packages fresh cauliflower florets

- 1 package refrigerated diced potatoes with onions
- 2 cans unsalted chickpeas, rinsed and drained
- 1/2 teaspoon kosher salt
- 3/4 cup torn fresh basil leaves
- 1 cup plain 2% reduced-fat Greek yogurt
- 8 lime wedges

Methods
Melt butter in a large Dutch oven over medium-high heat.

Add onion and garlic; sauté 4 minutes.

Stir in curry paste, ginger, and cumin; cook 1 minute.

Stir in soy sauce and coconut milk; bring to a boil. Layer beans, cauliflower, potatoes, and chickpeas in pan; bring to a boil.

Cover; reduce heat, and simmer 10 minutes. Stir in salt.

Stir in basil, or follow freezing instructions, below.

Place 1 3/4 cups stew in each of 8 bowls.

Top each serving with 2 tablespoons yogurt and 1 lime wedge.

Freeze:

Cool prepared meal completely. Cover with foil; freeze up to 2 months.

Spiced Chicken Casserole

Ingredients
- 2 cups water
- 6 black peppercorns
- 1 large garlic clove, crushed
- 1 bay leaf
- 1 3/4 pounds skinless, boneless chicken breasts
- 3/4 teaspoon kosher salt
- 5 ounces Monterey Jack cheese, shredded and divided
- 4 green onions, thinly sliced
- 1 cup chopped fresh cilantro
- 1 1/2 pounds fresh tomatillos, chopped
- 1 can chopped green chiles, undrained
- 1/4 cup half-and-half
- 2 ounces 1/3-less-fat cream cheese, softened
- Cooking spray
- 15 corn tortillas, halved
- 1/2 cup quartered cherry tomatoes
- 1/4 cup cilantro leaves

Methods

Preheat oven to 350°.

Bring 2 cups water, peppercorns, garlic, and bay leaf to a boil in a large saucepan.

Add chicken to pan; reduce heat and simmer, partially covered, 15 minutes or until chicken is done, turning after 10 minutes.

Place chicken on a plate; cool slightly.

Remove garlic clove from pan; reserve. Shred chicken with 2 forks.

Place chicken, salt, 3 ounces Monterey Jack cheese , and green onions in a bowl; stir to combine.

Place reserved garlic clove, cilantro, tomatillos, and chiles in the bowl of a food processor; process until finely chopped.

Add half-and-half and cream cheese; process until smooth.

Coat 2 square glass or ceramic baking dishes with cooking spray.

Spread 1/2 cup tomatillo sauce in the bottom of each dish.

Arrange 5 tortilla halves over sauce in each dish; top each dish with one-fourth of chicken mixture.

Repeat layers once, ending with tortillas and remaining tomatillo sauce.

Sprinkle evenly with remaining 2 ounces Monterey Jack.

Bake at 350° for 15 minutes.

Continue baking at 350° for 10 minutes, or remove 1 dish from oven and follow freezing Directions.

Divide each dish into 4 pieces.

Place 1 piece on each of 8 plates; sprinkle evenly with tomato and cilantro leaves, if desired. Serve immediately.

Freeze:

Cool prepared meal completely. Cover with foil; freeze up to 2 months.

Sausage Calzones

Ingredients

- 1 1/2 pounds refrigerated fresh pizza dough
- 3 tablespoons extra-virgin olive oil, divided
- 1 tablespoon tomato paste
- 2 teaspoons minced garlic
- 4 cups chopped seeded tomato
- 1 1/2 teaspoons sugar
- 1/4 cup chopped fresh basil
- 2 teaspoons oregano
- 8 ounces mild turkey Italian sausage links, casings removed
- 1 cup chopped onion
- 2 cups diced red bell pepper
- 1/4 teaspoon freshly ground black pepper
- 1/8 teaspoon kosher salt
- 1/4 cup yellow cornmeal
- 4 ounces part-skim mozzarella cheese, shredded
- Cooking spray

Methods

Let the dough stand, covered, at room tem-per-ature 1 hour.

Preheat oven to 450°.

Heat 2 tablespoons olive oil in a medium saucepan over medium heat.

Stir in tomato paste and garlic; cook 1 minute.

Add tomato and sugar; cook 10 minutes, stirring occasionally.

Stir in basil and oregano. Keep warm.

Heat a large nonstick skillet over medium heat.

Add 1 1/2 teaspoons oil to pan; swirl to coat.

Add sausage, and cook 6 minutes or until browned, stirring to crumble.

Place sausage in a bowl. Add remaining 1 1/2 teaspoons oil to pan.

Add onion, bell pepper, black pepper, and salt to pan; cook 5 minutes.

Add pepper mixture to sausage.

Line 2 baking sheets with parchment paper, and sprinkle with cornmeal.

Divide dough into 8 equal portions.

Roll each portion into a 6-inch round on a lightly floured surface.

Top each round with about 2 tablespoons sauce, leaving a 1/2-inch border.

Top rounds evenly with sausage mixture and cheese; fold dough over filling, and crimp edges with a fork to seal.

Arrange calzones on prepared baking sheets; coat with cooking spray.

Bake at 450° for 15 minutes. Bake an additional 10 minutes, or follow freezing instructions.

Top each calzone with about 2 tablespoons sauce.

Freeze:

Cool prepared meal completely. Cover with foil; freeze up to 2 months.

White Beans With Pork

Ingredients
- 1 cup dried white beans

- 6 cups boiling water

- 1 1/2 tablespoons olive oil, divided

- 1 (1-pound) boneless pork picnic roast, cut into 1/2-inch pieces

- 1/2 teaspoon salt, divided

- 1/2 teaspoon black pepper

- 2 cups fat-free, lower-sodium chicken broth

- 1/2 cup water

- 2 fresh thyme sprigs

- 1 fresh sage sprig

- 2 cups coarsely chopped onion

- 1/2 cup coarsely chopped carrot

- 6 garlic cloves, coarsely chopped

Methods

Place beans in a Dutch oven; cover with 6 cups boiling water.

Let stand for 1 hour; drain.

Preheat oven to 325°.

Heat a Dutch oven over medium-high heat.

Add 1 tablespoon olive oil to pan, and swirl to coat.

Sprinkle pork evenly with 1/4 teaspoon salt and pepper.

Add pork to pan; sauté for 6 minutes, turning to brown on all sides.

Stir in beans, remaining 1/4 teaspoon salt, broth, and next 3 Ingredients ; bring to a boil. Cover and bake at 325° for 1 hour.

4. Heat a skillet over medium-high heat.

Add remaining 1 1/2 teaspoons oil to pan; swirl to coat.

Add onion and carrot; sauté 4 minutes, stirring occasionally.

Add garlic, and sauté 1 minute, stirring constantly.

Stir onion mixture into bean mixture; bake at 325° an additional 1 1/2 hours or until beans are tender.

Drain solids through a sieve over a bowl, reserving solids and cooking liquid.

Skim fat from top of liquid; discard fat.

Stir cooking liquid back into pork mixture.

Freeze:

Cool prepared meal completely. Cover with foil; freeze up to 2 months.

Vegetarian Empanadas

Ingredients
- 9 ounces all-purpose flour
- 3/4 teaspoon kosher salt
- 1/3 cup canola oil
- 1/4 cup cold water
- 1 tablespoon cider vinegar
- 1 large egg, lightly beaten
- 1 poblano chile
- 1 tablespoon cumin seeds
- 1 cup mashed cooked sweet potatoes
- 1 cup canned black beans, rinsed and drained
- 1/3 cup chopped green onions
- 2 tablespoons chopped fresh cilantro
- 1 teaspoon ancho chile powder
- 1/2 teaspoon kosher salt
- 1 egg white, lightly beaten

Methods

Weigh or lightly spoon flour into dry measuring cups, and level with a knife.

Combine flour and 3/4 teaspoon salt in a large bowl, stirring with a whisk.

Combine canola oil, 1/4 cup water, 1 tablespoon vinegar, and egg in a medium bowl.

Gradually add oil mixture to flour mixture, stirring just until moist.

Knead lightly until smooth.

Shape dough into a ball, and wrap in plastic wrap. Chill for 1 hour.

Preheat broiler.

Place poblano on a foil-lined baking sheet; broil 8 minutes or until blackened, turning after 6 minutes.

Place in a paper bag; close tightly. Let stand 15 minutes.

Peel chile; cut in half lengthwise. Discard seeds and membranes. Finely chop.

Preheat oven to 400°.

Cook the cumin seeds in a large saucepan over medium heat 1 minute or until toasted, stirring constantly.

Place cumin in a clean spice or coffee grinder; process until ground.

Combine cumin, poblano, sweet potatoes, and next 5 Ingredients in a large bowl; mash with a fork until almost smooth.

Divide dough into 10 equal portions, shaping each into a ball.

Roll each dough portion into a circle on a lightly floured surface.

Working with 1 portion at a time, spoon 3 level tablespoons poblano mixture into center of each circle.

Moisten edges of dough with egg white; fold dough over filling.

Press edges together to seal.

Place empanadas on a large baking sheet coated with cooking spray.

Cut 3 diagonal slits across top of each empanada.

Bake at 400° for 16 minutes or until lightly browned.

Freeze:

Cool prepared meal completely. Cover with foil; freeze up to 2 months.

French Onion Soup For Slow Cooker

Ingredients
- 1/4 cup unsalted butter

- 6 thyme sprigs

- 1 bay leaf

- 5 pounds large sweet onions, vertically sliced

- 1 tablespoon sugar

- 6 cups unsalted beef stock

- 2 tablespoons red wine vinegar

- 1 1/2 teaspoons kosher salt

- 1 teaspoon black pepper

- 24 slices whole-grain French bread baguette

- 5 ounces Gruyère cheese, shredded

Method

Place butter, thyme, and bay leaf in the bottom of a 6-quart electric slow cooker.

Add onions; sprinkle with sugar. Cover and cook on HIGH for 8 hours.

Remove thyme and bay leaf; discard.

Add stock, vinegar, salt, and pepper; cook, covered, on HIGH for 30 minutes.

Preheat broiler to high.

Arrange bread in a single layer on 2 baking sheets; broil 30 seconds on each side or until toasted.

Place 1 cup soup in each of 12 (8-ounce) ramekins or ovenproof bowls, or follow freezing instructions.

Top each serving with 2 bread slices and about 2 tablespoons cheese.

Place 6 ramekins on a jelly-roll pan; broil 2 minutes or until cheese melts and begins to brown.

Repeat procedure with remaining 6 ramekins, bread slices, and cheese.

Freeze:

Cool prepared meal completely. Cover with foil; freeze up to 2 months.

Easy Minestrone Soup

Ingredients

- 2 tablespoons olive oil
- 2 cups thinly sliced leek, white and light green parts only
- 1 cup thinly sliced carrot
- 1 cup thinly sliced celery
- 2 large garlic cloves, minced
- 2 tablespoons tomato paste
- 8 cups unsalted chicken stock
- 1 (14.5-ounce) can unsalted diced tomatoes, undrained
- 1 (14.5-ounce) can unsalted cannellini beans, rinsed, drained, and divided
- 2 cups chopped yellow squash
- 2 cups chopped zucchini
- 1 cup chopped red bell pepper
- 1 cup fresh green beans, cut into 1-inch pieces
- 1/2 cup uncooked ditalini pasta
- 3/4 teaspoon kosher salt
- 1/2 teaspoon black pepper
- 5 ounces Lacinato kale, stemmed and chopped
- 1/4 cup pesto
- 2 ounces Parmesan cheese, grated

Methods

Heat a large Dutch oven over medium heat. Add oil; swirl to coat.

Add leek, carrot, celery, and garlic; cover and cook 5 minutes, stirring occasionally.

Add tomato paste; cook 2 minutes, stirring constantly.

Add stock and tomatoes; bring to a boil. Reduce heat to low, and simmer 15 minutes.

Place 1 cup cannellini beans in a small bowl; mash with a fork.

Add mashed beans, remaining cannellini beans, squashes, bell pepper, green beans, pasta, salt, and black pepper to pan.

Increase heat to medium; cook 10 minutes. Stir in kale; cook 2 minutes.

Place 2 cups soup in each of 8 bowls, or follow freezing instructions.

Top each serving with 1 1/2 teaspoons pesto and 1 tablespoon Parmesan cheese.

Freeze:

Cool prepared meal completely. Cover with foil; freeze up to 2 months.

Sausage - Sage Soup

Ingredients
- Cooking spray

- 2 cups chopped onion

- 1 cup chopped fennel bulb

- 1/2 to 1 teaspoon crushed red pepper
- 20 ounces hot Italian sausage links, casings removed
- 8 garlic cloves, minced
- 1/4 cup chopped fresh sage
- 1 tablespoon tomato paste
- 1 cup dry white wine
- 6 cups unsalted chicken stock
- 2 cups chopped plum tomato
- 4 (14.5-ounce) cans organic cannellini beans, rinsed and drained
- 1/4 cup chopped fresh flat-leaf parsley

Method

Heat a large Dutch oven over medium heat. Coat pan with cooking spray.

Add onion and next 4 Ingredients (through garlic); cook 3 minutes.

Reduce heat; cook 10 minutes or until sausage is browned and vegetables are tender, stirring to crumble sausage.

Add sage and tomato paste; cook 1 minute, stirring constantly.

Add wine; cook 3 minutes or until liquid is reduced by half.

Add stock; bring to a boil, reduce heat, and simmer 5 minutes.

Add tomato and beans, and cook 2 minutes.

Sprinkle with chopped parsley, or follow freezing instructions.

Freeze:

Cool prepared meal completely. Cover with foil; freeze up to 2 months.

Charming Chicken

Peanut Chicken Curry

Serves: 4

Ingredients:

4 pieces chicken breasts or thighs

2 cups coconut milk

1 tsp. curry powder

1 tsp. red curry paste

½ tsp. honey

⅛ tsp. red pepper flakes

2 Tbsp. peanut butter

2 Tbsp. tamari sauce

½ bulb large onion

½ large red bell pepper

2 large basil leaves

¼ cup cilantro

1 cup snap or snow peas

For garnishing: lime, cilantro, chives and toasted cashews

Method:
1. Place coconut milk, curry powder, curry paste and honey in freezer-safe container, mix to combine.
2. Chop onion, bell pepper, basil and cilantro into bite sized pieces, add to curry sauce.
3. Stir the curry sauce to ensure ingredients are combined properly.
4. Add chicken, ensuring the chicken is completely covered by the sauce.
5. Seal container and freeze.
6. When ready to cook, thaw the chicken curry and cook in a crockpot on low for approximately 5-6 hours. Serve over rice.

Prunes With Chicken

Serves: 4 – 5

Ingredients:

2 pounds chicken breasts or thighs

2 bay leaves

3 minced garlic cloves

2/3 cup halved pitted prunes

¼ cup capers

¼ cup olive oil

¼ cup red wine vinegar

2 Tbsp. dried oregano

Pinch of salt

½ tsp. pepper

½ cup apple juice

Method:
1. Combine all ingredients in a freezer-safe container.
2. Seal container and place in freezer.
3. To cook, remove from freezer and thaw.
4. Place ingredients in crockpot and cook on high for 3-4 hours.
5. Serve with roasted vegetables.

Teriyaki Chicken

Serves: 6 – 8

Ingredients:

6-8 Chicken Thighs

1 cup gluten-free teriyaki sauce

1 cup water

2/3 cup brown sugar

3 cloves garlic

3 slices ginger

Method:
1. Dissolve sugar in water.
2. Place all ingredients into a freezer-safe container or plastic bag.
3. To cook, thaw for 1 hour at room temperature.
4. Cook in crockpot on low heat for 4-6 hours.
5. Serve with rice and salad.

Sweet Bbq Chicken

Serves: 4 – 6

Ingredients:

4-6 chicken breasts

12 oz. gluten-free BBQ Sauce

2/3 - 1/2 Cup Brown Sugar

¼ cup vinegar

1/8 tsp. of cayenne pepper

1 tsp. garlic powder

Method:
1. Rub chicken with cayenne pepper.
2. Add chicken and rest of the ingredients into freezer-safe container for freezing.
3. To cook, place meal in crockpot and set on low for 4-6 hours.
4. Serve with roasted veggies.

Dijon Chicken

Serves: 6 – 8

Ingredients:
6-8 pounds chicken thighs
1 cup Dijon mustard
½ cup maple syrup
2 Tbsp. red wine vinegar
Salt & pepper

Method:
1. Place chicken in freezer-safe container.
2. Mix together mustard, maple syrup, vinegar salt and pepper until combined.
3. Pour over chicken, seal container and freeze.
4. Ready to cook? Remove from freezer and place in crockpot for 4 hours on high heat.
5. Serve with mashed potatoes.

Garlic Lime Chicken

Serves: 6 – 8

Ingredients:

6-8 bone-in chicken thighs
1 cup tamari sauce
½ cup lime juice
2 Tbsp. gluten-free Worcestershire sauce
4 minced garlic cloves
1 tsp. dry mustard
1 tsp. ground pepper
2 Tbsp. cornstarch

Method:
1. Place chicken in freezer-safe container.
2. In a bowl, mix together wet and dry ingredients.
3. Pour sauce over chicken.
4. Seal container and freezer
5. Ready to eat? Cook in crockpot on low for 8 hours.
6. Serve with mashed potatoes.

Pineapple Chicken

Serves: 6 – 8

Ingredients:

2 cups sugar

½ cup tamari sauce

1 cup pineapple juice

1 cup gluten-free ketchup

¼ cup red wine vinegar
2 Tbsp. mustard
6-8 chicken breasts
2 – 16 oz. drained canned pineapple

Method:
1. Place sugar, tamari sauce, pineapple juice, ketchup, vinegar and mustard in a saucepan.
2. Cook over medium heat for 4 minutes, stirring to combine.
3. Take off heat and allow to cool.
4. Place chicken in freezer-safe container.
5. Pour cooled sauce over chicken, seal container and freeze.
6. When you are ready, cook in crockpot for 8 hours on low or 4 hours on high.
7. Serve over rice.

Chicken &Black Beans

Serves:**4**

Ingredients:

1 can of corn, drained

1 can of black beans, drained

16oz gluten-free salsa

2 pounds chicken breasts

8oz. cream cheese to serve

Method:
1. Place all ingredients except cream cheese into a freezer safe container for freezing.
2. When you are ready to cook, place frozen meal into crockpot and cook on high for 6-7 hours.
3. 30 minutes before serving the meal, remove chicken for shredding.

4. Chop up cream cheese into chunks.
5. Place the shredded chicken back into the crockpot along with the cream cheese to cook for the last 30 minutes. Serve over rice.

Bbq Orange Chicken

Serves: **4**

Ingredients:

4 chicken breasts
1 cup orange marmalade
1 cup of BBQ sauce
3 Tbsp. of tamari sauce

Method:
1. Place all ingredients into freezer-safe container.
2. Mix together until combined evenly, seal & freeze.
3. When you are ready, cook in crockpot for 4-5 hours on high heat.
4. Shred chicken when cooked and serve over rice with steamed vegetables.

Sticky Apricot Chicken

Serves: 4

Ingredients:

4 chicken breasts
1 cup barbecue sauce
1 cup apricot jam or preserves
1 packet gluten-free dry onion soup

2 Tbsp. water

Method:
1. Combine all ingredients in a freezer-safe container.
2. Mix ingredients together well, seal and freeze.
3. When ready to cook, place in crockpot for 3-4 hours on high.
4. Serve over rice with steamed veggies.

Pleasant Pork

Pepper Pork

Serves: 4 – 6

Ingredients:

4 to 6 pork loin chops

1 onion cut in chunks

2 cloves minced garlic

2 seeded bell peppers cut into chunks

1 x 15 oz. can diced tomatoes

3 Tbsp. gluten-free Worcestershire sauce

½ tsp. dried thyme leaves

Salt and pepper to taste

Method:
1. Season pork with salt & pepper.

2. Place all ingredients in a freezer-safe container, seal & toss gently to distribute ingredients.
3. When you are ready, place the frozen ingredients in a crockpot for 6-8 hours on high.
4. Serve pork with some rice and hot sauce if you like a spicy kick.

Bbq Baby Back Ribs

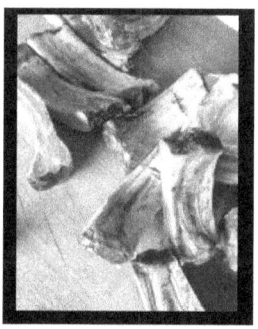

Serves: 5 – 6

Ingredients:

2 Tbsp. paprika

2 Tbsp. packed brown sugar

1 Tbsp. kosher salt

1/2 Tbsp. ground black pepper

5-6 lbs. baby back ribs

2 cups gluten-free barbeque sauce

Method:

1. In a small bowl, mix together paprika, sugar, salt and pepper.
2. Rub this mixture into the ribs.
3. Place ribs into freezer-safe container and pour BBQ sauce on top.
4. Seal and freeze.
5. When you are ready, thaw the ribs for 24 hours.
6. Cook in crockpot for 4-5 on low heat.
7. Serve with roasted vegetables.

Ham Soup

Serves: 2 – 4

Ingredients:

2 cups diced ham

3 potatoes, diced

1 onion, diced

½ bag baby carrots

1 bay leaf

8 oz. chicken broth

Salt and pepper

+ 1 can of gluten-free creamy chicken soup

Method:
1. Combine all ingredients in a freezer-safe container, seal & freeze.
2. To cook, pour frozen ingredients into slow cooker.
3. Add in the creamy chicken soup.

4. Cook on low heat for 7-9 hours and serve with gluten-free bread.

Sweet & Sour Pork

Serves: 6 – 8

Ingredients:

2 pounds boneless pork, cut into 1" chunks

2 tsp. smoked paprika

1 tsp. salt

¼ tsp. white pepper

2 Tbsp. olive oil

2 onions, sliced

2 green bell peppers cut into chunks

16 oz. bag baby carrots

2 x 13 oz. cans pineapple chunks

1/3 cup vinegar

1/4 cup sugar

3 Tbsp. corn starch

1 Tbsp. tamari sauce

1/2 cup pineapple juice

Method:
1. Combine paprika, salt and pepper to rub on pork.

2. Place all ingredients into a freezer-safe container and stir together.

3. When ready, cook using a crockpot on low heat for 8-9 hours.
4. Serve with rice or couscous.

Honey Maple Pork Ribs

Serves:**6**

Ingredients:

1 x 10.5 oz. can beef broth

3 pounds baby back pork ribs

¼ cup maple syrup

¼ cup tamari sauce

¼ cup gluten-free barbeque sauce

½ cup water

¼ cup honey

3 tablespoons honey mustard

Method:
1. Place all ingredients into a freezer-safe container.
2. Seal and toss to combine ingredients evenly then freeze.
3. When ready, place ingredients in a crockpot & cook on high for 5-6 hours.

Sweet Soy & Ketchup Pork Chops

Serves:**6**

Ingredients:

6 boneless pork chops

2 cloves crushed garlic

1/2 cup ketchup

1/2 cup gluten-free soy sauce

1/2 cup brown sugar

Pinch of pepper

Method:
1. In a bowl, combine garlic, ketchup, soy sauce and brown sugar.
2. Stir to dissolve sugar and place in freezer-safe container.
3. Add pork to the container and make sure it's covered with the sauce.
4. Seal and freeze.
5. When ready, pour all ingredients into a crockpot and cook on low for 6 hours.
6. Serve with rice or potatoes.

Pineapple Pork Roast

Serves:**6**

Ingredients:

1.5cups chopped dried cranberries

1 x 20 oz. can pineapple chunks, not drained

1 tsp. ground black pepper

2 tsp.salt

1 x 3 pound boneless pork roast

Method:
1. Rub Pork with salt & pepper.

2. Place in freezer-safe container along with cranberries & pineapple chunks.

3. Seal and freeze for future use.

4. If you are ready to cook, place in crockpot for 7 hours on low heat.

Balsamic Pork

Serves: 8

Ingredients:

2 pound boneless pork shoulder roast

Salt, to taste

½ tsp. garlic powder

½ tsp. red pepper flakes

1/3 cup chicken broth

1/3 cup balsamic vinegar

1 Tbsp. Worcestershire sauce

1 Tbsp. honey

Method:
1. Mix together chicken broth, vinegar, Worcestershire sauce & honey.

2. Rub salt, garlic powder & pepper flakes on pork.

3. Place all ingredients in a freezer-safe container, seal & freeze.
4. When you're ready to cook, place in crockpot for 6-8 hours on low.
5. Serve with roasted veggies.

Ham & Corn Chowder

Serves: 8 – 10

Ingredients:

2 cubes gluten-free chicken bouillon

Salt and pepper to taste

2 tablespoons melted butter

1 15.25 oz. can whole kernel corn, undrained

3 stalks celery, chopped

2 cups diced ham

2 onions, chopped

5 potatoes, peeled and cubed

+ 1 x 12 oz. can evaporated milk

Method:
1. Place all ingredients in freezer-safe container except evaporated milk.
2. Seal & freeze to use when desired.
3. When you're ready, place frozen ingredients into a crockpot.

4. Cook for 8-9 hours on low, then add the milk and cook for another 30 minutes.
5. Serve with gluten-free bread.

Vegetable Pork Stew

Serves:**6**

Ingredients:

2 cups baby carrots

1 pound small red-skinned potatoes

1 x 14.5 oz. can diced tomatoes, drained

1.5 pounds thick cut boneless pork chops

1 can 24 oz. gluten-free garlic & herb pasta sauce

1 Tbsp. sugar

+ 1 x 14.5 oz. can cut green beans, drained

Method:
1. Leave the skin on the potatoes and quarter them.
2. Chop boneless pork chops into 24 pieces.
3. In a freezer-safe container combine tomatoes, pasta sauce & sugar.
4. Add in potatoes, baby carrots & pork.
5. Seal the container and freeze for future use.
6. When you're ready, place ingredients in crockpot and cook on low for 8-9 hours.
7. Stir in the can of green beans just before serving.

Beloved Beef

Sloppy Joes

Serves: **6**

Ingredients:

1.5 pounds ground beef
1 cup finely chopped onion
2 cloves minced garlic
¼ cup finely chopped green pepper
½ tsp. salt
½ tsp. pepper
1 tsp. dry mustard powder
½ cup chilli sauce
14 oz. can tomato sauce
2 Tbsp. ketchup
1 Tbsp. brown sugar
2 tsp. gluten-free Worcestershire sauce
2 tsp. lemon juice

Method:
1. In a pan brown the ground beef.

2. Combine beef and all ingredients in a freezer-safe container.
3. Seal and freeze to use at a later date.

4. When you are ready, cook in a crockpot for 3 hours on low.
5. Serve on gluten-free bread.

Spicy Shredded Beef

Serves: 6 – 8

Ingredients:

2.5 pounds boneless beef chuck

14.5 oz. chopped tomatoes, with juice

7 oz. spicy salsa

1 x 4 oz. can diced jalapeño chillies, drained

1 chopped onion

3 cloves minced garlic

2 Tbsp. chilli powder

1 Tbsp. honey

2.5 tsp. kosher salt

1 tsp. ground cumin

2 cups beef broth

Method:

1. Place all ingredients into a freezer-safe container and combine.
2. Seal & freeze to use when you desire.
3. When ready, place ingredients into a crockpot to cook for 8-10 on low heat.
4. In the last 30 minutes of cooking remove the lid to thicken the sauce.
5. Remove beef from crockpot to shred.
6. Serve shredded beef in sandwiches with a salad.
7. Make sure to ladle some sauce over the shredded beef for extra flavor.

Amazing Beef Stew

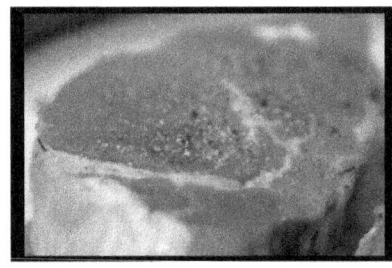

Serves:**6**

Ingredients:

2 pounds beef stew meat, cut into 1 inch cubes

4 sliced carrots

3 diced potatoes

1.5 cups beef broth

1 chopped onion

1 tsp. Worcestershire sauce

1 tsp. paprika

1 bay leaf

1 clove minced garlic

½ tsp. ground black pepper

½ tsp. salt

¼ cup cornstarch

Method:
1. Combine flour, salt and pepper then rub on the beef stew meat.
2. Place meat in freezer-safe container and stir in the rest of the ingredients.
3. Seal & freeze to use whenever desired.
4. Ready to cook? Place all ingredients in a crockpot and cook on high for 4-6 hours or low for 10-12 hours.
5. Serve & enjoy.

Mediterranean Brisket

Serves: 6 – 8

Ingredients:

2.5 pound flat-cut brisket

Salt and pepper

1 x 14.5oz. can diced tomatoes with juice

½ cup dry red wine

5 cloves chopped garlic

1/3cup black olives, pitted and chopped

½ tsp. dried rosemary

+ 1 Tbsp. finely chopped fresh parsley for serving

Method:
1. Sprinkle salt and pepper on brisket & place in freezer-safe container.
2. Add tomatoes, wine, garlic, olives & rosemary to meat and combine.
3. Seal and freeze to use later.
4. When you are ready, place all ingredients into crockpot and cook for 5-6 hours on high.
5. Sprinkle parsley on top and serve with mashed potatoes and steamed veggies.

Beef Stroganoff

Serves:**4**

Ingredients:

Salt and pepper

2 teaspoons paprika

1.5 pounds beef stew meat, cut into cubes

1 Tbsp. vegetable oil

6 oz. white mushrooms

3 thinly sliced shallots

1.5 cups beef broth

½ cup sour cream

Method:
1. Sprinkle salt, pepper & 1 tsp. of paprika of beef.
2. Heat oil in skillet on high and brown the beef by stirring for about 8 minutes.
3. Add in the remaining paprika, shallots & mushrooms, cook for 3 minutes.
4. Stir in broth and sour cream, cook for another 2 minutes.
5. Pour all ingredients into a freezer-safe container and allow to cool before freezing.
6. When you are ready, cook ingredients in a crockpot on low for 6 hours.
7. Serve with steamed vegetables.

Mozzarella Meatloaf With Mushrooms & Pepperoni

Serves: **6**

Ingredients:

2 slices gluten-free bread

1.5 pounds ground sirloin

1.5 cups finely chopped button mushrooms

1 cup shredded low fat mozzarella

1/3 cup finely chopped pepperoni

1 tsp. dried oregano

1 tsp. garlic powder

¾ tsp. salt

2 large eggs, lightly beaten

2 Tbsp. ketchup

Method:
1. Tear up bread and blend in food processor until crumbs are achieved.
2. Combine all ingredients in a bowl and use your hands to form a loaf that will fit in your crockpot.
3. Place loaf in freezer-safe container, seal & freeze.
4. If tonight is meatloaf night, put your premade loaf into the crockpot and cook on low for about 5 hours.
5. Serve with mashed potatoes & steamed veggies.

Pepper Steak Roast

Serves: **6**

Ingredients:

3 pound sirloin tip roast

1.5cups beef broth

¼ cup tamari sauce

1 red pepper

1 green pepper

2 small red onions

Ground pepper

1 garlic clove

Method:
1. Place sirloin roast in freezer-safe container.
2. Add in broth &tamari sauce.
3. Chop up peppers and onions, place on top of roast.
4. Add in pepper and clove of garlic.
5. Seal & freeze for later.
6. When ready, place ingredients in crockpot and cook on high for 4-5 hours.
7. Serve with your favorite steamed vegetables.

Beef Cocktail Cranberry Meatballs

Serves:**10**

Ingredients:

1 pound lean ground beef

8 oz. cranberry sauce

3 Tbsp. minced onion

½ cup gluten-free bread crumbs

2 Tbsp. water

1 egg

1 tsp. lemon juice

1 tablespoon brown sugar

¾ cup chili sauce

Method:
1. Preheat oven to 350°F on bake.
2. Combine beef, egg, water, crumbs & mince in a bowl.
3. Roll meat into small meatballs.
4. Brown meatballs on a skillet over high heat.
5. In a freezer-safe container mix together chilli sauce, cranberry sauce, lemon juice and sugar.
6. Place in browned meatballs and let cool.
7. Seal container and freeze for future use.
8. When ready to cook, place meatballs and sauce in a crockpot.
9. Cook for 1-2 hours on medium heat.
10. Serve with gluten-free pasta.

Beef Chili

Serves: **10**

Ingredients:

2 pounds lean ground beef

1/4 cup chili powder

1 x 46 oz. can tomato juice

1 x 29 oz. can tomato sauce

1 x 15 oz. can kidney beans, drained and rinsed

1 x 15 oz. can pinto beans, drained and rinsed

1.5 cups chopped onion

¼ cup chopped green bell pepper

1/8 tsp. ground cayenne pepper

½ tsp. white sugar

½ tsp. dried oregano

½ tsp. ground black pepper

1 tsp. salt

1.5 tsp. ground cumin

Method:
1. Brown beef in large skillet over high heat until brown.
2. Combine all ingredients in a freezer-safe container.
3. Seal & freeze to use when you need to.

4. If it's chilli night, take out the frozen ingredients and place them in your crockpot.
5. Cook on low for 8-10 hours.
6. Serve with gluten-free bread.

Beef & Veggie Curry

Serves: **8**

Ingredients:

2 Tbsp. oil

3 pound gravy beef, cut into 1 inch cubes

2 sliced brown onions

½ cup gluten-free curry paste

1.5 pounds potatoes, unpeeled, cut into 1 inch cubes

½ cauliflower, cut into small florets

2 cans diced tomatoes

1 cup beef stock

1 cup frozen baby peas

Method:
1. Combine all ingredients in a freezer-safe container.
2. Seal & freeze for later.
3. When ready, cook in a crockpot on low for 8-9 hours.
4. Stir the curry after 4 hours.
5. Serve with steamed rice, plain yogurt & coriander.

Superb Seafood

Seafood Chowder

Serves: 9

Ingredients:

4 chopped slices bacon

1 chopped onion

2 cloves minced garlic

6 cups chicken stock

2 large potatoes, diced

3 stalks celery, diced

2 large carrots, diced

Ground black pepper

1/2 tsp. red pepper flakes

1 cup scallops

1 cup raw medium shrimp, peeled and deveined

1/4 pound bite-size pieces of halibut

1 cup fresh corn kernels

1 x 12 oz. can evaporated milk

Method:

1. Cook bacon, onion and garlic in skillet over high heat to brown.
2. Place all ingredients in freezer-safe container and combine.
3. Seal container & freeze for later.
4. When you're ready, place the frozen chowder mix into a crockpot and cook for 4-5 hours on high heat.
5. Serve & enjoy.

Scrumptious Shrimp & Chicken

Serves: 4 – 6

Ingredients:

2 pounds chicken cut in chunks

2 tsp. of vegetable oil

¾ cup chopped onion

2 cloves garlic, minced

¼ cup parsley, minced

½ cup white wine

12 oz. tomato sauce

1 tsp. dried leaf basil

1 pound uncooked shrimp, peeled and deveined

Method:
1. Brown chicken, onion & garlic in a frying pan with vegetable oil over high heat.
2. Combine all ingredients in a freezer-safe container.

3. Seal and freeze for later.
4. When ready, place in crockpot to cook on medium for 4-5 hours.
5. Serve with rice or couscous.

Citrus Fish

Serves:**6**

Ingredients:

1.5 pounds fish fillets

Salt and pepper

½ cup chopped onion

5 Tbsp. chopped fresh parsley

1 Tbsp. vegetable oil

2 tsp. grated lemon rind

2 tsp. grated orange rind

Method:
1. Sprinkle salt and pepper on fish.
2. Place fish, onion, parsley, oil, lemon and orange rind in a freezer-safe container.
3. Seal and freeze to cook when you desire.
4. When you are ready to eat some citrus fish, place the frozen ingredients in a crockpot for 2 hours on low heat.
5. Garnish with some lemon slices and parsley sprigs and serve with rice.

Shrimp & Chicken Jambalaya

Serves:**8**

Ingredients:

1 pound shrimp, cooked

1 pound boneless chicken breasts cut in 1-inch cubes

8 oz. gluten-free smoked sausage, sliced

½ cup chopped onion

1 green bell pepper, chopped

28 oz. crushed tomatoes

1 cup chicken broth

½ cup dry white wine

2 tsp. dried leaf oregano

2 tsp. dried parsley

2 tsp. Cajun seasoning

1 tsp. cayenne pepper

Method:
1. Combine all ingredients into a freezer-safe container.
2. Seal and freeze to cook when needed.
3. When you decide to eat this jambalaya, place ingredients in a crockpot and cook on high for 3-4 hours or on low for 8-9 hours.
4. Serve over steamed rice.

Sweet & Sour Shrimp

Serves: **4**

Ingredients:

6 oz. frozen Chinese pea pods

14 oz. pineapple tidbits in juice

½ cup reserved pineapple juice

2 Tbsp. cornstarch

3 Tbsp. sugar

1 cup chicken broth

1 Tbsp. gluten-free soy sauce

1/2 tsp. ground ginger

16 oz. frozen medium shrimp, cleaned and cooked

2 Tbsp. cider vinegar

Method:
1. In a saucepan combine corn starch, sugar, pineapple juice & chicken broth over medium heat until sugar is dissolved and a thick sauce is formed.
2. Allow the sauce to cool.
3. Place all ingredients into a freezer-safe container, seal and freeze.
4. If you are ready for sweet & sour shrimp, then place the frozen ingredients into a crockpot and cook for 3-5 hours on low heat.
5. Serve over hot steamed rice.

www.ingramcontent.com/pod-product-compliance
Lightning Source LLC
Chambersburg PA
CBHW071436070526
44578CB00001B/103